£2

THE
ENGLISH
AND
THEIR HORSES

THE
ENGLISH
AND
THEIR HORSES

Libby Purves and Paul Heiney

Photographs by Kit Houghton

THE BODLEY HEAD
LONDON

To Kate, for the idea, and to David M.,
for the encouragement

A CIP catalogue record for this book
is available from the British Library

ISBN 0 370 31175 2

© Libby Purves, Paul Heiney & Kit Houghton 1988

Printed and bound in
Great Britain for
The Bodley Head Ltd
32 Bedford Square
London WC1B 3EL
by Butler & Tanner, Frome and London
set in Sabon
by Wyvern Typesetting Ltd, Bristol

First published 1988

Contents

Introduction

Nobody knows how many horses and ponies there are in Britain; or how many horse-owners. And despite any vague idea that outsiders may have of "horsy people", many of the men, women, and children in this book would barely recognize one another as belonging to the same fraternity. What has the Duke of Edinburgh in common with a truculent child horse-trader, bareback and sweating at Appleby Fair? What links a film star with a retired miner, a marchioness with an elderly clergyman in a cowboy hat? What will you find in a borstal or a circus, in a barracks or at Woburn Abbey? The answer is, horses. They are everywhere, pulling ploughs or coaches, racing, jumping, performing, hunting, or just existing quietly in a field for the delight and comfort of their owners.

There is a great diversity of people in Britain who find joy in horses; it is this joy and this diversity which we set out to celebrate. We found a beautiful Suffolk mare bloomingly in foal in an East Anglian winter landscape, surrounded by inmates of one of HM's penal colonies; we photographed Solomon in his glory in the mews at Buckingham Palace, little Noddy the Shetland covered with thistles in a rough paddock, and Troy the circus-horse cantering faithfully round a sawdust ring with a family of fake Red Indians on his back. We heard the story of the horse who tried his hardest to buck off a ceremonial trumpeter of the King's Troop, of Major Ronald Ferguson's tiny pony Pudin who has defied 100 mph balls for eleven years, of brave hunters, eccentric coach-horses, and pretty little show-ponies. In the course of our travels throughout the country we would meet such legends as Mrs Moss, Regal Realm and Aldaniti, then find ourselves being kissed and nuzzled by a totter's old pony or sharing a quiet moment by a campfire with an itinerant gypsy's nag. We tried to find out what kind of people take to showing, or dressage, or eventing; who makes detailed equestrian sculptures and who does hand-stands on the backs of these wonderful, ever-patient animals. There are worlds within worlds in horsemanship; there is coach-driving and there is manure-carting, breeding and racing and jumping and ploughing and just plain showing-off.

We asked all our subjects to choose one horse or pony, the best and dearest one, to talk about; and we came out of it all with a new respect for all horses and ponies. And for the people whose lives they have, slowly but surely, taken over. Our thanks to all of them.

Kit Houghton, Libby Purves, Paul Heiney
1988

THE ROYAL BAY:

HRH *The Duke of Edinburgh and Solomon*

"Of course," muttered the royal equerry, "he will be wearing his official uniform." We were standing in the courtyard of Buckingham Palace waiting for the Duke of Edinburgh to appear.

"Er, which particular uniform will His Royal Highness be wearing?" I murmured.

"I meant the *horse*," said the equerry, at which point Prince Philip—wearing a suit—appeared and bustled us round to the Royal Mews, the London home of all the Queen's horses. And there, in the courtyard, amidst the gilded splendour of the Coronation Coach and shimmering state harness and decorations, stood Solomon, in all his glory. He stood to attention, his uniform immaculate. Gold braid edged his stable rug, a regimental badge embroidered in heavy red and golden threads ensuring that it was never going to be blown away easily in a gust. His blackened hooves sparkled as brightly as any pair of parade boots, but that was only to be expected of a horse wearing the uniform of the Colonel-in-Chief of the Grenadier Guards. He clearly wore it with pride.

But Solomon has other reasons for pride. This Cleveland Bay-thoroughbred cross has not spent his entire working life in the cosseted luxury of royal stables. He's been out in the field, and seen a thing or two. "He's a survivor," said the Duke, giving him a hefty pat on the shoulder and fondly adjusting his forelock. Prince Philip, a fearless and experienced team driver, had chosen Solomon as his favourite out of all the past and present teams he has driven in competition.

He gave me a tour of the horse's various honourable scars. "That cut there"—a lengthy scar dangerously close to Solomon's eye—"happened in a driving competition. He was one of my wheel-horses [working nearest to the carriage in a team of four] and we got into a bit of a muddle in a hazard. One of the horses in front of

him started to kick out and he got cut." The Duke leaned forward. "That scar on his leg. That was another driving accident with me ..." And so the inventory of twenty-year-old Solomon's scars went on, each inflicted in the course of four-in-hand driving contests, a sport of which Prince Philip was founding father.

It began in the early 1970s. Finding that increasing age was making polo-playing more difficult, the Duke found his imagination caught by a fledgling sport called carriage-driving. At the time, he was president of the FEI, the international governing body of equestrian sport, and so in a good position to have driving-competition rules drawn up—modelled on the three-day event which tests ridden horses. There is a dressage test, a cross-country drive ending in a series of tight hazards to be negotiated, involving trees and fences, water and inconveniently placed oildrums and—at one Sandringham event—flapping Windsurfer sails for the horses to go between. Finally, there is the equivalent of the showjumping arena: a maze of traffic cones which neither horses nor carriage-wheels must knock over. The competitions flourished, helped by his association and constant participation in it; today it is the fastest-growing of all the equestrian sports.

Of course, all the horses that the Duke of Edinburgh needed for his own teams were to be found in the Royal Mews. Until then, they had been largely confined to ceremonial duties. It must have been something of a shock for Solomon and the rest to be taken from dignified processions and flung into the exhausting and dangerous world of carriage-driving where, judging by the scars, there is much thrust and not a little cut.

"But it's intelligence you need in a carriage horse," said the Duke. "Solomon is extremely strong, and obviously that's a help, too. If I had a criticism I would say that he's over-strong. He was always a bit too enthusiastic, too eager. I think he tried too hard." He paused, looked at the horse and smiled. "He probably got me into more scrapes than he got me out of." A laugh, another hefty pat. Solomon didn't flinch. They're kindred spirits.

They've been together in ceremonial events, too. Every year, at the Trooping the Colour ceremony on the Queen's official birthday, it has been Solomon that the Duke has chosen to ride from Buckingham Palace to Horse Guards Parade. "It's the variety that keeps him interested," says the Duke. "A change is good for him. That's why the horses here are put to a variety of uses." And that is why they also have to exhibit a variety of temperaments: one week Solomon might be asked to charge headlong across muddy tracks and thread himself through intricate, twisting driving hazards with all his strength and enthusiasm; the next, he will have to take his master in stately fashion down the Mall.

"I remember the first year that I rode him at Trooping the Colour. He was very interested, and liked to see everything that was going on. An amusing horse in many ways. He was quite happy just to stand around; he used to keep his eyes half-shut, just watch the parade and take it all in. Yes, a very amusing horse. A bit aloof, as well. The other horses in the Mews will come rushing for food, but he won't rush. He's quite happy to take his time. He doesn't want to be at the front. He's a modest horse in many ways."

He paused, and looked the horse in the eye. "Heart as big as a bucket, as well!"

Now their partnership is over. Solomon will not be seen again on Horse Guards Parade, nor in the carriage-driving events in which, the Duke admits, "It's getting too difficult to keep up, these days." He will retire to a field, probably at Hampton Court. But it has been a good combination of man and horse. Both of them, in their individual ways, have spent their working lives following, strongly, a few paces behind.

THE TOTTER'S PONY:

Digger and Snowy

Underneath the concrete pillars of the Westway, the busy urban motorway that drains London on its western side, there is a quite unexpected stableyard. There is a lot of stored scrap metal, some homemade carts, and a few chickens scratching around as the traffic thunders overhead. Snowy lives here, tended by his master, Digger: he is one of the few totters' ponies still working in the capital. "Totter" is the right word, these days: some call them rag-and-bone men, but in these affluent times it is scrap metal that interests the trade more keenly than rags or bones. Like benevolent urban parasites grooming their huge scruffy host, the totters collect unwanted wheel-hubs, old prams, discarded radiators and the other obsolescent detritus of modern London, and gainfully recycle it.

Digger (christened Samuel Williams) is keen on recycling. Take a close look at the wheel of his cart and you will recognize the spokes of a 1920s taxi, cushioned by a modern motorcycle tyre. Observe Snowy's bridle, and the tarnished initials UD show up: it used to belong to United Dairies. His collar, and his spare collar, both came off a skip in the road. In fact one of the things which most annoys Digger, both as a horseman and a scavenger, is the thought that so much perfectly good harness was wantonly burned in the Fifties when farms became mechanized. "Bonfires, they made of it. It's a disgrace."

His father was a totter before him. "I went out with my Dad, and I didn't want any other life. No two days are ever the same." There was no question of modernizing and mechanizing. "No point. In a van, you're going faster, you don't see things so much or spot people waving at you, and you're all closed in. You have to observe a lot in this job, and sit nice and high up. A horse and cart is perfect. Besides, it's company." Now he's one of the sights of London; he's

even been a television extra on *Minder*. When Snowy appears, clopping down the road on his extra-thick flat shoes (to avoid wear), people come out with sweets and apples for him and, if Digger is lucky, also feel inclined to search out a few nice lumps of scrap iron for the cart. In his dad's day, a particularly good haul would be rewarded with a goldfish in a plastic bag, carried slung under the cart, but he doesn't bother any more. The rare, old-fashioned sight of the pony and cart is reward enough for most people.

Digger's beat is West London—Kensington, Chelsea, Fulham, and Barnes—and Snowy has some pretty high-class admirers there. "Lord Snowdon always gives him something to eat," says Digger with a nonchalant sniff. Certainly, he is a beguiling pony even in his scruffy working state. He is ten years old, and was found eight years ago in Norfolk by his master, starved to the bone. "But I could tell it was the treatment that was wrong, not the horse." Digger took him to the vet, and brought him to London. "But he was too weak to work. No way I could take him out like that." Eventually he became strong enough to replace old Ginger, his chestnut predecessor, and took on a five-day week "with the odd week's holiday out in the yard to give him a breather". He's been a success. "He's intelligent, but nice and passive. Just what you need. He'll stand still outside a caff for ages, even if I don't chain the wheel. And he can hear the rustle of a sweet packet anywhere. Hoy—Snow—" Digger tested Snowy's reflexes, creeping around with his Polo packet: the pony's white head followed him, unhurriedly, confident of his eventual sweet. "Only thing he's frightened of is steamrollers. But I'll tell you one thing he *won't* do, just won't learn it: Ginger used to come when I called him, move further up the road or whatever. Snowy won't. He says, 'No, mate, you come to me.' So I do."

Digger's mate is Tony, the son of his father's late partner. The generation gap is apparent in the fact that Tony wears quite a smart donkey-jacket, and Digger prefers the voluminous old wool overcoat of tradition and a pair of plastic trousers "to keep the draughts out". They pause in fixing their wheel to demonstrate Snowy's affectionate nature. "This horse," says Digger impressively, "will kiss you. Properly." Tony ducks his head under the pony's nose and Snowy, after a moment's thought, stops eating his bran and

delivers a perfect smacking kiss with his whiskery white lips. "See?" Digger puts out the back of his hand, and Snowy kisses that, too. Then I lean over and offer my cheek: the pony, with aplomb, delivers a rather branny, but very gentle, munching kiss to my ear, then glares around for a Polo mint. "You're a soft thing," says Tony. Digger looks on approvingly for a moment, then backs the pony out into the road.

There is a long day ahead for Snowy: trotting the empty cart through the streets, calling for scrap; standing patiently while the men manoeuvre their booty aboard; moving on again, standing again, waiting with a nosebag outside a steamy café. It will be dusk before he comes home, at a slow, heavy walk, to the stable underneath the roaring motorway that leads to Badminton, to Gatcombe Park, to the green hunting shires. Other places, other horses.

Still, one day Snowy will be retired to a green field of his own, somewhere. It's all planned. "Well, I wouldn't do the other thing," says Digger.

THE PRISON PUNCH:

Bruce Smith and Colony Orchid

Few of HM prisons are set so bleakly or so beautifully as the Hollesley Bay Colony, so named after its beginnings as a colonial college for "young gentlemen intending to become colonists" to learn the business of farming. Today, as a prison, it falls into two halves: a secure unit for young offenders, and a more relaxed Youth Custody Centre. Perched on the eastern edge of Suffolk, at the far end of a long narrow lane, it is surrounded on three sides by water. When someone misguidedly tries to abscond from it, said one prison officer, "it's not long before we get a very wet lad back". The setting is beautiful, and rural, but presents a desperately bleak prospect to those boys whose misdeeds have been set against the crowded colourfulness of the inner cities: they quake at the hoot of an owl or the call of a fox, and stare fearfully into the misty, marshy distances.

But Hollesley is also a farm, supplying meat and milk for other prisons, and it is a famous Suffolk Punch stud. Indeed, such is the resurgence of interest in farm horses that most of the Hollesley foals now also find billets within the prison service. And in charge of the stud, as relaxed and benevolent as one of his own horses, is Bruce Smith.

"I was at Rochester before this, on the prison farm. I taught myself the horse work, and the first time I harnessed a horse, I did it with a book in one hand; first time I ploughed I was all over the place. But I've never been afraid to ask. When I came to manage the stud, I got a lot of help from the vet, Mr Ryder-Davis, and from other people—Roger Clark for instance. I always ask advice of everyone." The policy has paid off: his animals—or rather, Her Majesty's animals—now carry off trophies at every show, and the foals which don't stay in the prison farms find eager buyers. Bruce has now been at the stud eight years. "I tell the boys that, when they

complain about doing eight months . . ." He breaks off to direct one of his young grooms to hold a yearling's head for our picture. "That's right, move round, we're not going to show your face" (a prison stipulation). "Just as well, really, it's not a horror book." The boy grins, and retires behind the young horse's soft brown neck.

All the assistance at the stud is provided by inmates: boys come there to work who have never met a horse before, and Bruce has to ease them into it. "They report on my doorstep, very rarely knowing anything at all, and usually never having had a job. That's a big change since I've been working in the prison service: fifteen years ago, any boy who came in had had some sort of a job, sometime—and knew about work. Today they've usually been on the dole since school. So I give them a little talk about the stud, then put them on sweeping and general work, so they're used to working around the horses. Some are very nervous because of the size of them, but gradually you see their confidence building; eventually they can lead horses, take them to the field and so forth, then groom them . . . within a few months they're out in harness with the cart, or even driving one with the big sweeping machine behind."

Considering that in the rest of the equestrian world it is taken for granted that a groom is a mad keen, rather underpaid enthusiast— generally a girl—Bruce's position is unique. But his unlikely horsemen sometimes throw up joyful surprises. "One went on to be a farrier. I saw him at a show, in a shoeing competition and he said, 'Hey, remember me?' Some go to farms, but really there isn't much work in this line for anyone. But for years, lots of them will come up to me at shows, dressed up as Hell's Angels or whatever so I don't recognize them, and say, 'Hello Bruce', then to the horses, 'Hello Timber. Hello Orchid . . .'"

Baffled, rather carping media representatives occasionally ask the prison service what on earth is the point of giving delinquent city boys a training in farming, especially with heavy horses? What have Suffolk Punches to do with modern youth training? Bruce defends the idea indignantly: he thinks they have quite a lot to offer.

"Think about it. For one thing it gives them something interesting, something alive. For another, a stable teaches you a work routine; and thirdly, what's important is the fact that working with animals, having other creatures relying on you, is the best way to learn responsibility." Watching the tender care with which one boy, a third-time recidivist who'd "lived in squats all his life" handled a big brown colt, I could see that the Suffolks must be giving the boys something. It is not hard to imagine, without undue

sentimentality, that if you are young and have had a chaotic,
loveless childhood and an outlaw adolescence, it might be a
hopeful thing, a healing thing, to meet a big, placid, soft-breathing
animal who does not judge or condemn you or even notice your
purple hair. "Well, you can sort of relax around them Suffolks,"
says Bruce. "It's hard work, of course, but you can always just lean
on one for a while, and have a chat." Selected boys go out to shows
with Bruce, camping in the horsebox and enjoying the freedom of
the showground. "And I never have any trouble, or hardly ever.
Nobody's escaped, either, though we don't take a warder with us."

The mother of the stud is Colony Orchid, a splendid twelve-
year-old brood mare. When we met, she was carrying her seventh
foal, due on Leap Year's Day 1988 and therefore presumed to be
lucky. She has won the working cart-horse class at most of the
shows in her time; she won the Royal at three years old, and was
Champion Suffolk at the Royal Norfolk in 1986, receiving a cup

from the Queen herself. Her foals are all finely shaped, as beautiful and soft and friendly as she is. Her son Timber is the sort of horse who ambles straight up to you in the field and eats your flowered skirt before you know it; she herself prefers knocking off Bruce's hat. From her velvet nose to her exceptionally pretty, pale, spreading tail, Orchid is all grace and friendliness. "And a good worker. We keep our mares working until a month before they foal, or until they can't fit in the shafts any more, whichever's the sooner. She's very nice, very easy to handle." Sure enough, ten minutes after I had leaned on her soft side and felt her foal kick and turn inside her, Orchid was plodding off in the shafts again, bound for the fields on her plate-sized feet.

"They were going to send her off to another prison this year," says Bruce. "I said no, hang on—you've other horses you can send apart from her. She has good foals, she's a natural in the show ring, likes to show herself off; she's never been ill once, and only been slightly lame on one occasion, at Framlingham Show. She doesn't owe us anything. Let's keep her here. So we did."

THE EVENTER:

Lucinda Green and Regal Realm

"There are not many horses that make me go weak at the knees," said Lucinda Green crisply. Looking at her taut athletic frame, boyish cropped hair and direct eye, it is hard to imagine anything making her weak at the knees, ever. She combines the authority of a head girl with a curious streak of wildness, even recklessness; she has been a top horse trials and three-day event rider for so long that she appears invincibly professional. But this formidable person hesitated for a moment in her swift, efficient wrapping up of Christmas whisky bottles to glance up at me and add vehemently, "But Regal Realm has always been special. Usually, the horses I have here are exercised by different people, but I can remember periods of not letting anyone else ride Regal Realm. If anything had happened to him, I wouldn't have wanted to blame anyone for it except myself."

She won the World and the European championships on Regal Realm, before his retirement at Burghley in 1987. An event horse is asked for three skills: dressage, showjumping in the ring, and a strenuous and often dangerous cross-country course, crossing deep water and leaping formidable obstacles to make clever landings and scramble across uncertain ground on the other side. Many horses can be taught dressage to the right standard, and show-jumping is a skill on its own, disciplined and precise; but the cross-country is at the heart of eventing, and if a horse can't do that well, there is no point letting him near it. As another top rider, Virginia Leng, once observed, "There are very few brave horses born." So an event rider looks first and foremost for a horse that will be safe, and brave, and clever in the cross-country; then teaches it the other skills. The answer does not always lie in top breeding, and certainly not in good looks.

When Lucinda first saw Regal Realm, it was at the "alternative

Olympic" contest in Fontainebleau, in the year of the Moscow Olympic boycott. "The Australian riders are noted for having to sell their horses at the end of an event, to pay their expenses for getting them there. And it was my Australian husband, David, who told me I ought to think about this horse. He was a cattle horse, who'd been worked to the bone on cattle stations, then became a reserve for the Australian Olympic team. So I went to see him do his dressage test. Well, there was this weedy brown horse, not very good-looking at all—and he wasn't very good at dressage, either—but he reminded me of Village Gossip, another horse I had which was bad at dressage but brilliant across country. In the end, I tried him—he jumped a crowd barrier and shot off into the countryside, and I thought, Wow!"

She bought him, and brought him home, whereupon he went lame for a year with a ligament strain; but, recovering, began to show the same headlong form. He won the World Championship and Badminton when he was still quite green. "Just hurtled around over everything, wouldn't slow up for any fences at all. Actually, that Badminton sobered him up and he learned to be a bit steadier. But he just loves belting along, jumping anything that's in the way. I think that unlike dressage, cross-country is a natural desire in the horse that you can nurture and harness."

An eventer can sometimes draw genius out of the sort of horse that many other riders would never bother with. "The type of horse I like riding is—well, the sort of horse some people would find was no good at all. Not exactly dangerous, but sharp, aggressive, fearless; and also it *must* have brains. I can't ride my best on a horse that needs constant help. What I'm best at doing is nothing—just setting them up and balancing them, then letting them find their way over. I don't interfere too much; I have a poor eye for a stride, so I train them to see their own stride and take it."

This critical mixture of reckless spirit and high intelligence turned out to be present in Regal Realm. It is curiously echoed in his owner, too: hearing Lucinda talk about their training relationship ("You mustn't bore a horse") is oddly like hearing her account of her own childhood. "My parents had a very happy attitude: riding was considered to be for fun and enjoyment, they never put any pressure on me. They didn't urge me to ride, or push me. But if I did something at all, I had to do it properly and finish what I started. I went into eventing because I was a jack of all trades—not good enough for pure showjumping, which is incredibly accurate work, and not interested enough in dressage to be good." She was, however, although she does not say it, always personally brilliant at the cross-country phase—and so was Regal Realm.

"Dressage wasn't his best thing, poor chap. It really wasn't his fault, he did try and he did what he was told, but he was just the wrong shape. He was made like a taut elastic band in an upside-down banana shape—a horse should be rounded, not hollowed. He even jumped hollow, which isn't conventional. He had the athletic ability of a Rumanian acrobat to get himself out of trouble, though: I don't think he ever fell, and he never seriously hit anything either. Our partnership was only a bit rocky for a while at first because he went so fast, and pulled. But in the end I could ride him in a simple vulcanite snaffle, because we had learned to confide in each other. I learned how brilliant he was, and he trusted me." She paused to wrap another bottle of whisky and label it. "One thing, though, he always needed a very short martingale because he used to throw his head back and practically shove his ears in your mouth. A very odd shape, he was."

You sense that it is a bravura partnership that won't happen again: the young rider, headlong and joyful across country, met a horse with the same spirit as hers and won against the odds and despite the lack of fine technical skills in the dressage. Lucinda says regretfully, "I wouldn't take on another Regal Realm, with the lack of dressage paces"; she is, after all, a professional and a winner who likes to stay at the top. But the moment of Regal Realm's retirement was the end of an era, and had a sadness of its own.

"You think, as a horse gets older, that there must be an end in sight. He retired at sixteen, after I'd had him since he was nine, and the last thing I wanted was to feel the edge come off him. And I was right to do it now; at Burghley, he wasn't so fast. He got time faults on the cross-country. Curious, he felt just as fast, to me." He is not going to stay in a paddock at her pretty red-brick home at Appleshaw near Andover, though. She does not want him there as an old pensioner, an occasional hack; when we talked, he was about to set off for Australia once more, half a world away.

"He's like my husband, he always loved heat. He loved Los Angeles when the rest of us were wilting. I didn't want him to stay here, in this climate, getting arthritis in a damp field. He's going to friends of ours who have a big station in Queensland; he'll do some cattle work, and sometimes be paraded at events and so on. He might be bitten by a black snake next week, and die; but I wouldn't want him to have a dull retirement here."

She will see him about once a year. It will probably not be too sentimental an occasion. "I'd be delighted if he did recognize me, but he isn't a horse who ever gives you an overwhelming feeling of recognition. He knows who his mates are, but he's very self-sufficient. When he used to have his holiday every year, out at grass, he didn't want anyone near him, even me, and didn't want to be caught, he just went into a wild state. One of the reasons he was

Above At the Waterfall Fence, Fairbanks Ranch, 1984 Olympic Games in California.

always so brilliant was that he was independent; when he was young he was a cattle-horse, and nobody had mollycoddled him; he lived hard, worked hard, he had to dodge craters and avoid black snakes. Even after years here, if he trod on one end of a twig and it flipped up he would rear away from it with an old protective reflex. He was always the sort of horse who looked after himself, the sort you can't own. You played it on his terms. No, I'm glad he's going to Australia. I would hate to think of him standing around in an English field, getting cold and wet and miserable."

THE COACH-HORSE:

John Parker and Pandur

John Parker drives horse teams: it follows that the horses in his stables have to be team players. In the idiosyncratic business which he and his partner, Susan Townsend, have built up in the last two decades, a useful horse is a versatile horse: one who will serve in the riding school, pull John's magnificent mail coach in the Lord Mayor's Parade, stand through a day's dull film work, or trot for miles on a marathon reconstruction of the Bristol-to-London mail coach run: a horse who can compete to world standard in the FEI carriage-driving championships, but pull a hearse at a funeral or a bride to a wedding with equal aplomb. In displays, John expects his team to gallop through arches of fire, turn on a sixpence, then wait placidly while a hectic band of Pony Clubbers dressed as mounted mice seethe around them in an Olympia Christmas finale.

His Hungarian greys live as a community, and work in chopping, changing teams of four and sometimes five. With one exception, the same horses are used for riding lessons in the school John and Susan run at Swingletree Stables near Diss; but even so, they have become so accustomed to teamwork that they won't consent to go out of the front gate singly. They like their mates to be with them, preferably trotting alongside. There are always new horses being brought on at Swingletree, and old ones gradually retiring on to light duties; so there are always about fifteen almost identical white heads peering over various stable doors next to Susan's Connemaras and Welsh ponies. It seemed invidious to ask John Parker to talk about any one favourite horse out of this tightly-knit team.

But he will. There is one, a Hungarian-thoroughbred cross, who is unlike any other. "Not like any horse in the world. I'll never find

one like him." It is Pandur, pronounced Panda, a sharp sixteen-year-old with the bones, a recent X-ray revealed, of a horse ten years his junior. John found him ten years ago, and has used him for preference as his nearside lead horse ever since. Was Pandur so good, then, from the beginning? "No," says his owner lovingly. "He was a bugger. You see, he's too sharp. Got four horses' brains in one horse's head, the memory of an elephant. He's a thinker. A devil. And my grandfather, who was a horseman, always said to me that a clever horse is a horse that will get you into trouble. Well, he was right. With anyone else, Pandur might be real trouble. But we get on."

John panders, as it were, to his favourite's little ways. "I get no pleasure out of fighting horses." So Pandur's kingly little routines go undisturbed: he is a horse who loads himself up the ramp into the horsebox, turns, gets into his own accustomed slot at the back and peers out until the ramp goes up before turning to his hay-net. "There's no point making him do unimportant things your way, just to put your authority on him. With a horse like Pandur, you have to respect his position in life. I only put my foot down about things like turning the wrong way at junctions."

This can be a challenge. John doesn't like being distracted with too much chat from his coach passengers when Pandur is in the lead, quivering with excitement at the end of the long reins. This horse is the modern embodiment of the old Arab proverb, "The camel-driver has his thoughts, and the camel he has his." He makes his mind up with lightning rapidity, and acts on impulse. "He'll try to turn left, for instance, because he's got it in his head that left is the way to go. So he tries, and you straighten him up, and he chucks his head down and rolls his shoulders around like a little boy who's been naughty and knows he looks silly. He'll sulk. He'll pretend he doesn't want to turn left anyway. Then the next left turn, wham! round he goes." To make things worse or, as John sees it, more challenging, Pandur's partner Gyorgy will turn too. "He's brainwashed her by telepathy." The sulk evaporates only when he does something right, and clever, and gets a few cheers from the crowd. "Then he stops sulking and puts his ears forward again." Pandur's ears are generally forward: other lead horses in teams bend theirs back, to catch the driver's muttered instructions — Pandur is rarely listening, but questing ahead for the next bit of fun. "His whole life is wanting to do things. His head's always out over the stable door, always; he knows if he's going on a trip, he knows if it's a long one or a short one, God knows how; and if you aren't taking him he'll bang his stable door and give trouble."

It doesn't do, John says, to rehearse Pandur before an event. "He's too sharp. We went to deliver a letter to the Queen at

Plymouth with the mail coach. Rehearsed the whole thing, but on the day they held us up five minutes longer. I tell you, Pandur was up there completely disgusted from the moment things didn't run to the second; he was really sending me a letter, saying get on with it, you've messed it up."

Pandur knows a lot. He knows London backwards. He could bring himself home from St Paul's to Buckingham Palace, says John (John's horses are often stabled in the Royal Mews), "and as for Norwich, we go there twice a year, once to open the courts with the Civic Coach, once to do the Lord Mayor. He knows the exact route: if I turn off it, he stops dead and stares round at me."

All John's horses have to be superlatively good and quiet in crowds, or there would be horrifying accidents. "People come up, pat them, shove them, pull their tails, grab their legs. People are not sensible about horses, they think a coach and four horses is the same as a lorry, that it's got brakes and can't go sideways. But Pandur is not afraid of anything. He's been through crowds in the pitch dark, through fire, been under Concorde taking off at Heathrow, gone right up to propeller aircraft at Birmingham, into tunnels, everywhere. You tell him to go, he'll go." And—a great asset to John's film and publicity work with the coach—Pandur always looks good: he is the one with his ears forward, after all, and his neck up, looking around, counting the house. The only thing John won't willingly take him out to face is a team of drum-majorettes. "He's a bit eccentric about drum-majorettes, especially if they're aged about five. He'll go forward, but be very frightened. It's because they're so small, and all feathery and fluffy. He thinks they're some sort of animal, I think."

Driving so often, and so intensely, for a living John revels in Pandur's abundant, eccentric character. Nothing is routine. "When he's not in the team, it all feels flat. Predictable. He's so clever, Pandur. You never know when he's going to have one of his sudden bright brainwaves, especially once the job's over and the cameras are gone. He'll play you up on the way back to the horsebox, amusing himself, doing everything right, but not quite right—stupid sharp turns and that sort of thing. He reckons he's just himself, and as far as he's concerned he's in charge of the lot of us. He can always find his way back to the horsebox after an event, even if you move it: I swear he smells it out, down the side-streets."

It is this borderline between brilliance and roguishness which intrigues the best horsemen in all fields. John wouldn't give Pandur to a pupil to drive without the tightest supervision. "He could be damn dangerous." But to onlookers, despite his temperament, Pandur remains sweetly harmless. Curiosity, not aggression, is his main characteristic. "He never fights the other horses, like all the rest do, and they don't fight him. I think perhaps he's no challenge to them because he's so different, nearer human than horse. He'd never hurt a fly, Pandur." John pauses there, then qualifies. "Well, he did black Susan's eye at the Lord Mayor's Show. But it was out of excitement. He just swung his head round and got her in the eye with the bit. He was trying to see something." He would be.

THE VICAR'S BRONCO:

Peter Birkett and Buck

I was invited to tea by the retired rector of Holford and Doddington, a small parish near the North Somerset coast. I found the church, as directed, and next to it a grand fourteenth- or fifteenth-century house. A grassy path ran from the rector's front door to an iron gate in the churchyard wall. It was very English, very Anglican, very reassuring. Then the Reverend Peter Birkett himself got out of his car. He did not actually say "Howdy, pardner," but he might well have done, because he was dressed more for the rodeo than for evensong: pointed leather boots, tight blue denim jeans, shirt with silver buttons, tasselled leather waistcoat. Over his arm was a cowboy saddle. "They think I'm mad around here, you know. Rector Rides Off Into Sunset, they say. Still, it gives them something to talk about. Would you care for tea?"

He extended his pastoral arm and took me into the hall of a magnificent house. "The fireplace was the last bit of modernization." He paused, "1572, I think." The roof was dark oak, vaulted and carved. His clerical robes hung from the walls; so did pairs of antlers, half-a-dozen cowboy saddles, and various ten-gallon hats; all part of this holy cowboy's collection. "There's nothing unusual, you know, in what I do. The very first ever cowboy was a Spanish Franciscan priest!" However, Peter Birkett is probably the only modern rector to have swopped a clerical collar for the spotted red neckerchief. And he *is* a cowboy, a real cowboy, not just someone who dresses up.

"Oh, I go out there for four months every year. I'm on my way to Arizona now. I work there. I was always interested in cowboys, since I was a boy reading comics, but never thought any more about it till my wife died. That was when I decided I wanted to loose myself. I set off for this place I had heard of in northern British Columbia. It was two hundred miles of dirt roads to get there, like in the pioneering days. There were moose to contend with, and grizzly bears. And no horrid humans. I loved it." His

speech slows to a drawl as he remembers every glorious moment of it. Then he sits up sharply. "I get infuriated by people's ignorance of cowboys, I could spit rivets. They say to me, 'Why do you want to go out to the Wild West?' I tell them London's a damned sight wilder. Cowboys are courteous and polite. There's no manners in England these days."

When he isn't out West, the horse that he rides across the imagined prairies and mountains of North Somerset is Buckshot, known as Buck. He does this more for practice than for sensation. "He's much too big for cowboy work, of course. What a working cowboy needs is really a cow-pony: a horse with real cow-sense. They know just what to do with a cow, so all you have to do is hang on. When I'm in California, I ride an Appaloosa called Shadow." He didn't learn to ride in any of the carefully tended riding schools or down the leafy lanes of Somerset. "No, I didn't learn at all. I was just put on a horse and got on with it. When I came home, I

couldn't believe the way things are: they just make riding such hard work in England. You'd never find a cowboy rising to the trot!'' In cowboy America, he explains, ''They ride them like motor-bikes. And always on a loose rein. You're riding with your legs, really. It's dressage, polo pony stuff, Spanish School all in one.''

Peter Birkett is no fantasist; he does not go on adventure holidays, he insists on living and actually working as a cowboy. ''I've tried roding''—catching cattle by throwing a loop in the end of a rope over the animal's head, you must never, he says sternly, call it lassooing. ''That's quite difficult. You've really got to start as soon as you can walk. They have plastic cows' heads stuck on an oildrum with four wooden legs, and they practise on them. I can throw a rope quite well now if I'm standing still, but not at full gallop.''

We wandered into the rectory kitchen, another repository for enough bullwhips and ropes to bring in a herd of charging steers. ''Cowboys are very vain,'' he said, pointing to the row of a dozen ten-gallon hats. ''They always like to have the latest fashions. These''—he fingered some leather half-trousers—''are chaps. You need them to stop the cactus ripping your legs.''

The kettle came to the boil. Peter Birkett sat down with a comfortable creak of his leathers. ''I usually go and work with the same crowd of people. The first time I went there they said if I ever wanted to go again, I could.'' His face broadened into a smile. ''They paid me one of the greatest compliments possible, you know. They said, 'Preachin' ain't changed you into a lily!' That's what I'd like on my tombstone. Tea?''

THE RIDING STAR:

Anthony Andrews and Spotty

Anthony Andrews has very frequently been cast as an English aristocrat of the old sort. He was the dissolute golden boy Sebastian in *Brideshead Revisited*; he was the abdicating King Edward VIII in *The Woman He Loved*; he was Sir Percy Blakeney in *The Scarlet Pimpernel*. His looks are classic, his manners faultlessly well-bred. All he needs to complete the image is a horse: perhaps a thoroughbred chestnut hunter, or a discreet grey hack.

Maybe that is why he has such a predilection for wild-looking coloured or spotted horses, like his beloved Appaloosa, Spotty. For nothing irritates Anthony Andrews so much as his typecast image, and the suggestion that his horsemanship is an image-booster. Indeed, it was only in tribute to Spotty and his qualities that he posed for us on horseback—if a morning's wild jumping over a pile of logs in his country garden can be considered to be posing. At showjumping events, where he competes fairly regularly, he makes great efforts to avoid the local press and not to be Anthony Andrews, the star. "It makes me angry," he says, "when the two things cross over. Riding is part of private life, and family life. I have been around horses since I was eight years old."

It began quite by chance. His mother was widowed, and poor, and "somehow she talked me into a tiny private school in Hendon. The headmistress was Mrs Williams, who I'm happy to say I am still in touch with; and her daughter Jane arrived to teach art. I loved art and I loved Jane, and she had a pony called Beam. She gave lessons at two and sixpence an hour. It was a struggle finding the money, but I went once a week or so. She and Beam taught me to ride in a very classical way."

He had an aptitude, and ended up by getting a useful reputation and therefore a lot of rides on other people's more challenging ponies. He did gymkhanas and trials, and told his mother that he would either be a showjumper or an actor. Acting won, and when he met his wife Georgina, who had formerly been a very promising showjumper and tipped for the British team, he had barely ridden at all for ten years. "I'd been travelling round the country, in rep, struggling away." Georgina, however, who had also given up competing for acting, still had two of her old horses and he took to riding one called Wotsisname, alias Fred, another coloured horse. The old love returned. Soon he was taking part in the lighthearted celebrity showjumping events at the Olympia Christmas Show, using his riding skills to good effect in films, and—when Fred died at twenty, mourned by all ("our marvellous groom Lynda was devoted to him")—he began to think of having a horse of his own.

"So one day, about two years ago, I got back from filming in Australia after a twenty-two-hour flight, staggered into the house wanting my bed, and was told by Georgina to go down to the stables with Jessica [his young daughter]. I grumbled, but I went down and Jessica flung open the door, and there was this spotted creature looking out at me." Its name was Dad's Spot: an eight-year-old Appaloosian gelding with several showjumping credits; his friend Ted Edgar had found him specifically for Anthony Andrews, Georgina had approved of him and bought him, and within a few paces his new owner fell in love.

"He just seems perfect for my personality, somehow. I always know within a few paces whether I'm going to get on with a horse; I've actually got off one almost immediately, because I didn't like the feeling. But Spotty is tremendous." This does not mean that the horse is quiet or easy. "Oh, no. He's no mug's ride. Not a horse I'd put a weekend guest on. He can be very, very difficult, extremely fast, and it needs a lot of confidence to ride him. But he gives me a fantastic feeling, and he loves his job and loves the showring; and when you're out hacking he'll jump over everything in sight for fun. I'm fairly cautious about physical risks usually, and the only exercise I do is riding; but when I'm on a horse, what I've discovered about myself is that I'll attempt things most people wouldn't."

He is not bragging. There is documentary evidence, on film, that given a horse to ride or to drive, Anthony Andrews doesn't easily hand over to a stunt-man. "My work means that I've had a chance to meet horses in all walks of life and all corners of the world, and I've had the luck to spend a lot of time on horseback. In *Ivanhoe*, I rode Fury, a marvellous Andalusian black stallion, the one in the Lloyds Bank advertisement. We could do anything together. And there was a race scene in *The Scarlet Pimpernel*, when I rode a French horse straight off the track: the camera crew were in a little Citroen 2 CV with the doors off, and I warned them they'd never

keep up. They wouldn't listen, but in the end they had to. I gave them a half-a-mile start." That was the film in which he drove a pony and cart, pursued by twelve horsemen with guns. "They'd got an old cart, because the script said 'old cart'. I wasn't sure about it. At one point I was standing with one foot on the shaft and one in the cart, the camera car driving ahead of me and the twelve horsemen galloping behind. I had to move my foot to stamp on a switch which exploded the flash wired up my arm, to show I'd been hit by a bullet, and as I did it the wheel fell off the cart." He pauses, smiling reminiscently. "It was strange, I saw it rolling off across the field before I actually went down. Well, the camera car driver saw what had happened and was so shocked that he stopped dead. I couldn't, so we crashed into the car, and the horse shot off across the park trailing bits of wood. The twelve horsemen behind couldn't stop either, so they galloped over the lot. There was this silence while the dust settled, then everyone looked around for the leading actor . . ."

In the best traditions of British gung-ho and of the Scarlet Pimpernel himself, he was unhurt. And certainly not put off horses. That could never happen.

"They're marvellous. So intelligent, and they can do so much. I have to be away from home a lot, filming, and even though our groom, Gay, is marvellous, I do fret a bit about how I'll find Spotty when I get back because it always takes a while to get a horse going your way. But somehow I always feel at one with him, and we get back very quickly together. He's a tremendous ride. Perfect for me."

THE PIT PONY:

Ron Philips and Brownie

"Best thing for a horse is hard work, damned hard work," says Ron Philips. Brownie proves his point. At thirty-two years old, and after fifteen years down a mine as a working pit pony, Brownie can still muster enough spirit to keep Ron's daughter Sharon on her toes. "To be honest," says Ron, "he's a bit of a funny 'un. He wants to show off. I tell you, when you get hold of him, you've got a job to hold him."

It is a wonder that, with this chippy temperament, Brownie survived his working life: the principal rule for a pit pony operating in the dank and cramped conditions of a coal-mine was that it should never put a foot wrong or cause trouble. Ron worked down there himself, with the ponies, and remembers the rigours of the work only too well.

"I had forty-four years in the pit. I started when I was fourteen." There is a miner's croak in his voice, a reminder of nearly half a century's exposure to filthy, pervasive coal dust. "There was no training scheme or anything, they just showed you how to gang. Ganging was working the tubs that used to take the soil or whatever away from the coal face." These tubs, running on rails, were pulled by ponies: the pit ponies, who became a byword for hard work in bad conditions. "We had fifty ponies working underground with us. There was an ostler, one on each shift, and his sole job was to look after them. He used to see that the water barrels were taken down the pit, and he would feed them. They had hay chop, a bit of oats and some bran. And, do you know, them mangers were never empty, *never* empty. Very well looked after, them ponies. A blacksmith used to go down every morning, *every* morning, to check their feet; if a shoe needed putting back, he'd do it there and then."

The pit pony's work was tough, heavy and repetitive. He would haul trains of tubs to the surface with coal or debris, and bring them back empty to the coal face. It was work that called for a willing horse, but definitely not a spirited one.

"Pure breeds were no good at all," says Ron. "Them horses with thin fetlocks, they'd never take to pit work. There's too much blood in 'em. Ours came off the moors. They were hairy, rough old things when we got 'em, but we used to clip 'em and feed 'em and try and get them nice and sleek and fat. You wouldn't recognize them." Again, Ron reassured me emphatically that their mangers were "never empty, *never*". Clearly, in the dark world of the mine, men and ponies lived and worked as comrades. "You could nearly make them ponies talk, we knew 'em so well. I can still remember the names: Dart, Brisk, Sam, Thunder, Tiny, Silver . . . we could really talk to them ponies."

As soon as the ponies had been brought down from the sunlit moors and got accustomed to living in the glimmer of the underground lighting, they would be broken to harness. "That was a bloody heartache, I tell you. A bloody heartache sometimes, with a young horse," remembers Ron. "They had to be very sensible, you see. The worst thing was a pony that wouldn't settle into its collar. Instead of just leaning into it to take the load, it jumped forward, and that would have the tub off the road and then there'd be a hell of a mess. We never had any reins or anything, the ponies just had to learn to follow the rails."

An experienced pit pony—and some of them worked for decades—became cannily professional. "They knew so much. Suppose they were walking along the rails and they came to a set of points, and they didn't think the points were set the right way— well, they wouldn't go any further. Some of them used to be able to open doors with their heads. And if you wanted them to come back for any reason, all you had to do was shout 'Come again!' and they'd turn towards you."

The National Coal Board finally brought the last of the ponies to the surface in 1975. Brownie got his discharge a little earlier than that, in 1972. Ron's daughter Sharon was thirteen then, and bought him at a pit pony sale. Down the mine, there was little sentiment about the ponies' going, despite the companionship which had come before.

"I wouldn't say they were missed. Some of them had done a good stint, thirty years old, some were. But as they got older, one or two of them started to cough. And there were accidents, of course. I remember there was one pony, Major, who got buried under sixty tubs full of dirt. We kept two loose-boxes underground as hospital boxes. No, I would have said they were better off out of the pit."

There is a popular myth that pit ponies spent twelve months of

every year down the mines. But when the miners had their holidays, so did the ponies. "Yes, we used to bring 'em out for the miners' galas. Coming up, we had to put the ponies in the cage and put a 'bluff' over their heads. It was a sort of sack so that when the cage went up, they wouldn't be frightened by the brickwork going past. When we got to the top, we'd lead 'em into the field. When they got out there, you should have seen 'em! They'd kick, and buck, and gallop about like spring lambs. The only trouble was catching them again when the holiday was over. That was the problem: getting them down t'pit again."

Which might, of course, account for Brownie's unwillingness to be caught and held. How can he know that each time he is caught he is not going to be led back again to that stuffy subterranean world of dust and echoing noise and black danger? Perhaps nobody has convinced him, yet, that it is all over and the pit ponies are back in the sunshine for good.

THE POLO PONY:

Major Ronald Ferguson and Pudin

"At what age," asked Major Ronald Ferguson, fixing me with his sharp eyes beneath the famous bushy ginger eyebrows, "does a baby get some strength in its back and stop slouching?" I thought about six months. "Well, there's a picture of me on a horse in one of those wicker baskets, and I'm slouched. So that's how young I started riding. 'Bout six months. Been riding ever since. Fifty-five and a half years."

Major Ferguson gives the impression that once his back stiffened in infancy, he made sure he never slouched again. In any sense. He is a former regular officer in the Life Guards, Deputy Chairman of the Guards' Polo Club, Prince Charles's polo manager (and formerly Prince Philip's), and incidentally the father of another energetic redhead, Sarah Ferguson, who became Prince Andrew's bride, the Duchess of York. We talked across his businesslike desk at the Guards' Polo Club on Smith's Lawn, with the noble acres of Windsor Great Park spread out around us, and the office door standing open for shouted conversations between the Major and the girls in the outer office—about sponsorship arrangements, the organization of chukkas for the season, and the question of whether the British team need one set of team shirts or two. After a lifetime of association with the Royal Family, he treats interviewers with familiar, masterful ease: "Never listen to the first two questions. The third is the trick one." But he has an affable and authoritative way of doing business, and thoroughly approves of being able to do so in these particular surroundings.

"In the playing season, the joy of it is that I can leave all the bumf and frustrations and telephone calls of administering the Club, and within ten minutes I'm in my breeches and on a horse. And out there, all the steam gets blown off. The great joy in the days before

my daughter's wedding to Prince Andrew, when there were forty-five press calls on me every day, was to get out and play hard for fifty minutes. Nobody could interrupt me or pester me out there, and if they did they'd have got run over. I can thoroughly understand what a thing polo must be for the Prince of Wales today, and Prince Philip in former days: it's a perfect, quick escape. They'd arrive here and you'd see steam practically rising off their heads after a series of official functions, and they'd just play a fast chukka and feel relaxed again. I really don't know how I'm going to be when I have to stop playing and just do the administration."

Like many lifelong horsemen, Ronald Ferguson sees little point in merely "going for a ride". He likes to *do* something on a horse, and in polo he discovered his real vocation. "I used to do all the gymkhanas and awful stuff like that as a child—I remember one horrific little Shetland pony called Flying Flash, it used to stop dead at every jump—then I did all the usual stuff, hunter trials, hunting, point-to-points. But I joined the Life Guards, and got sent to the Canal Zone in 1954. One day the CO said, "You're playing polo tomorrow." I'd always liked ball games, cricket, squash and so on, where you have to co-ordinate yourself. Polo just had everything: horses as well as a ball. I wrote to my father and told him to sell my steeplechasers. Polo was it. I loved it all—the horses, the galloping, the speed, hitting the ball, the thunder and guts of it, and the team spirit. I like playing in a team."

The office is lined with photographs and drawings of polo players, nearly all of them caught at a dizzying angle of about forty-five degrees to the ground, with stick flailing overhead on its whippy bamboo shaft. Despite its socialite image, despite the crowds of Sloaney girls and languid young men who crowd Smith's Lawn in summer and delight in walking the field at half-time to tread in the divots of turf thrown up by ponies' feet, polo is not a sport anyone takes up lightly. It is not a game for cowards, human or equine. "Polo ponies have to be agile, able to go flat out for twenty-five yards, stop dead, and shoot off in another direction. They have to get used to the stick near their legs, and to body contact. You're allowed to ride off another player at an angle of not more than forty-five degrees, which can mean impact at thirty miles an hour. If a pony starts to shy off when another one approaches, that pony's had enough and you don't play it any more." Some ponies, amazingly, play on for years and seem to enjoy the rough speed of the game, protected by their knee-pads from the 100 mph impact of the ball (although they get hit on the bottom, Major Ferguson says, "and so do the players"). It clearly demands a special temperament. "There was one bay mare called Conga, the biggest bitch you'd ever meet. Impossible in the stable, absolutely vicious to everyone, hated exercise, but get your white breeches on and she was sensational. She had five legs. And Chupi, she was a small chestnut mare, only fifteen hands" (polo ponies go up to 15.3 as a rule). "She put her ears back all the time, and behaved like a bit of a cow. But she was fast and keen and good. Then a grey gelding of mine, Barraglette—he's an absolute sod. Totally human. Can get out of any stable you lock him in . . ."

Is a good polo pony then, I wondered, invariably a tough nut? Are none of them cuddly and amiable creatures? "Oh yes. Barraglette is. And my American mare, Pudin. We'll take her photograph. Really cuddly, nice animal, likes a lot of affection. She's a freak: only 14.2, but immensely strong, and I've played her for *eleven seasons*." A strong but small pony is a great find for a polo-player, since the shorter the stick, the easier the ball is to hit. A good

pony like Pudin, able to carry on season after season without going off form, also develops valuable ball-game skills. "The horse follows the ball with its eyes, knows when you're about to do a backhand but doesn't anticipate the change of direction and ruin your timing."

He likes winning. "I don't want anyone on any team of mine who says they just play for fun and don't care. I loathe losing, like poison. But I'm not a bad loser, that's different. After a match the team gets together immediately to discuss what went wrong, but when we've all calmed down we'll drink at the bar with the other team very happily." He reached a handicap of 5 — the top is 10, but very few have ever attained it — and admits that in his fifty-seventh year he is slipping. "4 last year, 3 this year. I don't mind going down the tree. In winter now, I find that after all the injuries I've had, my old bones and muscles just complain and insist I stop riding except in hot countries. But in summer, it's fine, and there are players older than me still playing. I suppose I shall have to stop sometime." He will be missed on the field. So will Pudin.

THE ARAB STALLION:

The Marchioness Townshend and Sky Crusader

In 1988—the seventieth anniversary of the Arab Horse Society, and looked forward to as a celebration year—a sad blow fell. Lady Townshend, former president, great breeder of Arabians and moving spirit, died in the spring. A few weeks earlier I had been to see her, resting on a sofa but still hoping for a summer's riding. Both she and her horsemanship, and the horses she bred, are worth commemorating.

You turn off an empty Norfolk road, through imposing iron gates, to enter the long driveway of Raynham Hall. It is an elegant house, family home of the Townshends since 1618 and remodelled in the Palladian style in the eighteenth century; the grounds are landscaped, the lake beautifully placed, and even the barns and outbuildings are unusually easy on the eye. The whole place is essentially English and elegant, refined and well-bred; a pleasure to look at.

It could hardly be a better setting for its horses. They too are elegant and refined, and bred to a hair. They pour across the park at an exuberant gallop, silken manes flying, eager to greet visitors. Even with the thick, woolly winter coats they have grown to compensate for the difference between cold Norfolk and the hot desert, they retain that impossible, slightly fey, Arabian elegance as they career joyfully around the park. They are a lovely sight.

Yet Arabs have, in the British horse world, a slightly dubious reputation. Part of the trouble is that like all specialist breeds of animals, pure-bred Arab horses attract a disproportionate number of slightly dotty and unreasonably obsessive owners. Also, a large number of them are only ever shown in-hand—never ridden or driven, but kept as competitive decorations—and therefore the breed has developed a basically undeserved reputation for being "spooky", skittish and unreliable in temperament; not a practical horseman's choice. Indeed, many British horsemen and women

hold stoutly that the Arab's one important contribution has been its part in the development of the English thoroughbred, and that pure Arabs are best left alone.

Ann Townshend, however, gave the lie to much of this. For one thing, she was clearly not remotely dotty; for another, she maintained a steady policy of breeding her Arabs for performance as much as for beautiful conformation. An Arab to her was, first of all, the perfect riding horse. "I wouldn't keep a bad-tempered mare, however beautiful she might be, and I would never, ever breed from a bad-tempered stallion." An Arab, she always said, should be a horse "fit to gallop across deserts with a king on his back"; but the galloping matters as much as the beauty.

"I was a small child, so I always got put on ponies. Then when I was fourteen, I had my first Arab mare. She was, to me, amazingly smooth, soft, and responsive—that was it." After she married the Marquis Townshend and came to Raynham she bought Nawarra, an Arab mare, as a riding-horse, "And as they were incredibly cheap in those days, for some reason, I bought another mare to keep her company on the journey, and that was Chimera." She hacked, hunted occasionally, and then put the two mares in foal "when I was having babies myself. It seemed a sensible idea. Since I had Arabs, I thought it would be nice to breed something special from them." But, as will happen among horse-lovers, the numbers at Raynham mounted up, and the moment came when, inevitably, "You just get a beautiful colt you want to keep. So you end up running a stud."

That colt was Sky Crusader: the first Raynham stallion, true founder of the Sky Arabian Stud. He was, his owner said simply, "Angelic from the first moment. He was Nawarra's grandson, and very special. Beautiful. And he passes on his best points to all his foals—his back, his lovely head. And his temperament. You see, unless they've been bred for show and weaknesses allowed to creep in, Arabs are strong, hardy, with very dense bone; and they're naturally sweet, charming, kind, clever horses. Treat them gently, and they're wonderful; interested, very easy to break, and wonderfully comfortable to ride. They balance themselves naturally, you don't have to school them to balance. I've been out hunting with a woman who kept saying, 'Ooh, I wouldn't ride an Arab, they're so spooky,' then I've sat there waiting on my own traffic-proof Arab in the middle of a field while her horse bolted off at the sight of five bullocks. I had to escort her back, still criticizing Arabs' temperament."

Crusader has had a varied career. He was British National Champion as a yearling in 1971, and top Veteran in 1987. He has been ridden in cross-country events, jumped in the ring, hunted

with the West Norfolk, and came second, after only five weeks' training, in the first ever Arabian race meeting in Britain when he was ten. "He loves everything that he does." His foals and their progeny are being ridden, raced and shown all over the country. "You can do anything with them. They're good for dressage, good for riding, hunting, everything. They're clever. I'm not a fanatic, I like lots of other kinds of horses, and I think it's a great mistake when people start to think Arabs are all that there is. But they do have a sweetness and easiness about them."

I walked alone, as I left, to see Crusader himself in his box. He was irritated at being kept late for his lunch, and put his ears back angrily at me; but his beauty is indisputable. Grey, with brown freckling on his finely chiselled head, and a dark slender nose set on a haughty neck, he is handsome and powerful and unmistakably an aristocrat. You don't keep aristocrats away from their lunch for long, so I moved on; his colt, Sky Desert, with the same head, came shyly up to nuzzle me; and a groom led out a beautiful, feminine dappled creature with elegant white socks for me to admire. Crusader's daughter, Sky Hera. "This is a special mare to her ladyship," said the groom. A new favourite, from the old stock.

Crusader, rather smugly, got on with his feed. Seventeen years old, and he still wouldn't look out of place in a desert, galloping, with a king on his back.

THE CIRCUS HORSE:

Michael Austen and Troy

In the smart little Big Top of Austen Brothers' touring circus, the grand finale of the performance is the arrival of the whooping, leaping, rope-spinning cowboy-and-Indian troupe known as the Eight Nevadas. To be strictly accurate, all but one of the Eight Nevadas are actually Austens: there is Michael Austen and his brother Patrick, Patrick's wife and daughter, and Michael's three daughters. The youngest is ten years old. When they have spun their ropes and done a bit of fire-eating, the Nevadas bring on their horse, Troy, a placid creature, "part Welsh cob, part something else". Troy's job is to canter clockwise round the ring with a hypnotically regular, utterly reliable gait, rather like a cross between a rocking-horse and a metronome. The Nevadas leap fearlessly on and off him, kneeling and standing and forming showy little three-man pyramids on his broad back, timing their jumps to his predictable swaying gait. And the children in the audience clap and cheer and laugh. Everyone loves cowboys-and-Indians, everyone thrills to trick-riding. The Indians are showy, the girls pretty, the spangles bright and the music stirring; but they couldn't do any of it without plain, reliable Troy.

Michael Austen was one of the pioneers who brought back touring circus to Britain on a regular basis. In the late Sixties, it is fair to say that circus here was dying on its feet: the big, famous shows were beginning to collapse under their own weight, and there were few small versatile companies to replace them. The Austens started a joint circus with Gerry Cottle—now a genial rival—and set strictly professional standards on a small scale. The Austens always wanted horses to be a serious part of the circus. They had grown up with them, as Michael recounts: "My eldest brother used to be caretaker of a riding school, ages back, and we younger ones used to go and help with the horses, and got to ride them bareback from the common, free, and muck out and groom. When we got into the circus, we bought some ready trained ponies,

a pair of Shetlands, then got four more Shetlands and found some books on how to train them. There are three books on circus horses—one on *haute école*, one on liberty horses, and one about *voltige* riding. We got these Shetlands to do a liberty routine, pirouetting, standing on pedestals, running in pairs, jumping. But no riding, of course." The third book, on the ancient art of *voltige*, or trick-riding, remained a tantalizing temptation. Eventually, two years later, "We went to a horse sale, and with us was this very famous man Ron Brewer—the Donkey King—and he saw this spotted stallion and said we ought to buy it for riding. So we did. Someone gave us an old roller and a bridle, and we set about teaching this horse, Prince, to run at a steady pace and all that. Well, we was learning, and the horse was learning, and we all got over the mistakes together. Slowly." Prince served under the pirouetting Indians for a decade, and was retired two years ago for a peaceful old age, out at grass at the circus's winter quarters near Swindon. But, says Michael sadly, "Three months later he died. I honestly think he missed it. My father is the caretaker at winter quarters, and he says that Prince kind of seemed to mope, really. He missed being loaded in the box, and travelling with the other horses. Circus horses know the routine; they always know when it's moving day, and they get excited. The last show they work in a location, they're really difficult—fast, over-excited—they know we're off again. Poor old Prince missed all that."

Troy came next; they found him on Dartmoor. "The moment I saw him, I knew he'd be good—he had this lovely regular gait, nice front leg action, like a horse that's trotted with a cart." They brought him to the circus and began the painstaking process of training him to walk, trot, and finally canter with perfect regularity, clockwise round the ring. After eight months, the Eight Nevadas were sure they had the right horse: calm in temperament, predictable in step. So they began jumping on and off.

"Think about it from the horse's point of view. With a horse that's never had anyone stand or kneel on his back, it's all new; so you take it very quietly, pat him, give him sugar, let him know when he has been very, very good. A horse gets very startled the first time you do a handstand on him. Well, he would. He's never seen anyone's legs up there, so when he looks back it's a shock. And when you stand up, and you canter past the light, this odd shadow of you will cross in front of him. And when you kneel on him, there'll be a tickling feeling he doesn't know, and he'll lurch forward." With patience, and advice from "a very good sea-lion trainer, Arthur Scott", Troy and the Austens learned new tricks together. Few things can spook Troy these days or put him off his stride: crowds, lights, elephants, performing llamas and frantically

waving candyfloss all leave him indifferent, calm and collected. He will canter on regardless in his circle with two adults and a child perched on his back. He trusts them.

They trust him, too. "Any day at all, we could break our backs. It's important he doesn't ever do anything unexpected. We are afraid, sometimes, before the act, because it's real, and a real risk. But the fear goes away when you're out there. It's fun—it's the big highlight of the day. Performing in the ring is the icing on the cake, for us. We enjoy everything about the circus, the moving, pulling down the tent, putting it up—but it's being in the ring that gives you the real thrill. That goes for Troy, too."

Troy now has a partner, a slimmer horse called Basil. They are learning to trot in step, side by side, so that various Nevadas can travel round the ring with a foot on each back. Basil is taking to it well, but Troy is slightly offended by being asked to change his routine. "He's an old sticker." The *voltige* riding manual has one or two tricks about which Michael is cautiously ambitious: "Back-somersaults from one horse to another. . ." Those will have to wait.

Every now and then, Michael saddles up Troy to do a bit of normal, respectable riding. But it has its drawbacks. For one thing, Troy doesn't like to go far from the circus tent and vans. For another, despite having been trained and lunged in both directions round the ring for the sake of his musculature, the horse knows perfectly well that *voltige* riding acts always operate clockwise, and therefore he prefers to go that way. Out on a ride, Michael Austen admits, it is virtually impossible to persuade him to turn left.

THE SHOWJUMPER:

Harvey Smith and Digby

A gritty, granite-jawed Yorkshireman, Harvey Smith has been a legend for twenty years, both for his performance in the show-jumping arenas of the world and for his alarming bluntness outside them. Seventeen years ago he made a famous V-sign during the British Jumping Derby, upsetting a judge and losing himself the £2,000 first prize for "disgusting behaviour"—though he got it back in the end. Sixteen years ago he bluntly said that Princess Anne wasn't good enough to ride in the Munich Olympics. The press got very cross, but as it happened he was right. She didn't go to Munich, but reached her peak for the next one, at Montreal. Then there were various minor controversies: an accusation, and exoneration, on a charge of mistreating a horse; a clash between his jumping career and his son's. Meanwhile, he took for a while to the professional wrestling circuit, and actually won quite a few bouts; at present he raises extra money by going on periodic tours with his one-man cabaret act, sitting telling jokes to entranced, but slightly wary, provincial audiences. He is the frequent despair of the media, since it is impossible to know in advance whether he will be charming and witty or glum and monosyllabic. Legends grow around him like coral: Harvey Smith, they will tell you, refuses to stable his horses, but keeps them roaming loose in yards, and just rides whichever one gets to the gate first when he whistles; Harvey Smith keeps a pet lion, which rides behind him across the York-shire moors, and so forth.

But at the heart of all the legends, and behind all the nonsense stories, lies one golden nugget of fact: Harvey Smith understands horses. *Really* understands them, in a way rare even amongst horsemen. Twenty minutes talking with him will yield more

insights than reading a dozen books. When you first ask him a general question like "What makes a good horse?" he will growl tersely, "It's gotta jump. If it doesn't jump, what's the point?" But persevere, and the gleams of gold begin to appear.

He started out at eight years old with a borrowed pony called Simon, doing a milk round in the morning and jumping in the afternoon. He bought his first horse, Farmer's Boy, for £33 and schooled him until he became, on this hitherto untaught horse, the top showjumper of 1959 at the age of twenty-one. "I started with nothing, on a horse that knew nothing," he says simply. He had been working on a building site, with his wife running a chicken farm to bring in £5 a week.

Today he is well-sponsored and successful, and keeps a large number of horses on his farm on Ilkley Moor, riding and schooling them daily with his wife Susan. But the doggedness and the Yorkshire sense of economy have won him a formidable reputation for not spending money on showy, readymade horses, but bringing on animals that nobody else bothers with. "I wouldn't say I'm lucky. I just persevere a bit longer than other people. I'll sit back and *think* about a horse, about how to improve him. If I only make one per cent improvement in a day, in a hundred days, that's a hundred per cent improvement. So long as I can see daylight, I'll carry on. Take an ugly horse, bad conformation, but he can jump; look at him jumping, and the point is that you see that conformation *isn't* bad after all. It's all working when he leaps."

He doesn't bother to look at the newer generation of talented showjumpers with envy, despite the money and expertise and training backup which some of them bring to the sport he joined with nothing. "I don't care. If they don't put the work in, they won't get there, so who's to envy them? I wouldn't expect anyone else to follow the road I took."

It is true that he keeps his horses roaming loose, in large yards rather than separate boxes; it is an important part of his philosophy. "People put showjumpers in stables because they're so nervous of owt happening to them. Stable's a silly place for a horse. In a yard they come out fitter and live better. They don't get these respiratory troubles or anything. The only drawback is you have to have really strong rugs on them, because they pull off each other's rugs all the time and rip the ends." He likes to see the horses larking and shoving and establishing their herd hierarchy, and, with his punishing schedule, he finds them easier and more effective to work out of a yard.

"Look at it. If you keep a horse in a stable, the first three quarters of an hour he's out he's thinking, 'Whoopee, I'm free!' and messing about. He blows off steam, wastes your time. In the yard, you see

them playing and boxing together as much as they want, looking around—but when you bring them out and get a saddle on, they just say, 'Right, boss—what do you want me to do?' " As for the story about Harvey leaning on his gate, deciding at the last moment which horse to take to a big event, the truth of that lies in his pitiless and discerning eye. "You can look at a horse and tell when he's ready. There's that look. He's just right. I know when he's right, and I don't like going into a ring on a horse that isn't."

He doesn't like to pick out any one horse as the greatest ever: he names Farmer's Boy, ("A very generous honest horse"); O'Malley; Seahawk; Harvester ("With even one per cent chance of getting over, he'd try a jump"); and the legendary Mattie Brown; all his winners. But "You're always looking for a new one. The next one"; so we photographed him on Digby, a pleasant young animal fresh from foxhunter trials who has jumped 7 ft for him and is progressing through "the silly classes", getting ready for the big shows. "A horse can improve up to seventeen years old, or until he gets careless. The best horses are made by accidents: they hurt themselves once, and never want to clout a jump again. I can't stand careless horses who don't give a damn what they hit." But he denies ever getting angry with a horse. "Not really. You can't expect them to do any more for you than they've got in them, and there's nothing worse than a horse who's afraid, and looks back at his jockey all the time. So I don't scare them." Nor would he pick out any one moment of all his successes which gave him the greatest pleasure; not even that V-sign moment when Mattie Brown became the first horse to win the Jumping Derby two years running.

"But I'll tell you that the great moment is any moment when you're winning a good class, and the hoss under you is giving his all. Generously. And you can't ask more of it. I've often thought as much of a horse that comes second or third or fourth, if he's just given you generously what he has to give." For a moment, he is neither dour nor difficult, but open and glowing as he thinks of the horses who were—his favourite word of praise—"generous".

So I pluck up the nerve to ask him about the lion story. Yes, he said. He did have a lioness once. "Oh aye, it were a nice little thing. Tanya, its name was. Came from a circus. Used to lie around in the riding-school, sleep under the jumps. It only went for a horse once, and got both barrels, wham, off of its back legs. That taught the lion a lesson, so it was safe round horses after that. Anyway, the lion died of cat 'flu in the end." It turns out, though, that Tanya never actually rode around behind him on his horse. "That must be one of those stories. People," he pauses briefly, pretending to be baffled, "tell stories about me, you know. They do."

Facing Page Harvey Smith on Shining Example in the Nations Cup at Hickstead in 1987.

THE DRAWING-ROOM HORSES:

Lady Fisher's Falabellas

If you drive a little eastward from Newmarket, where high-bred racehorses gallop through the morning mist, you will find another sort of stud entirely. The horses of Kilverstone, near Thetford, are bred as carefully as any Derby winner, but not for speed so much as for size. These are perfect miniature horses: the curious, contrived creatures known as Falabellas after Señor Falabella, an Argentinian rancher whose maternal grandfather (an Irishman called Newton, actually) once found a tiny, perfectly proportioned horse and decided to breed a pet from it for his daughter. This little stallion's origins remain murky, but he was the founder of the breed which came to be known as Falabellas. Wherever he came from, he carried a dominant gene of smallness which means that every time a Falabella is crossed with an Arab or thoroughbred, the foal takes after the smaller parent. True specimens are never over 34 inches tall; the three yearlings in our picture are 25 inches, lower than a hall table.

We could tell that they were lower than a hall table, mainly because Karla, the dark grey, made straight for her mistress's fine walnut drum table when she trotted in, and began to scratch her quarters vigorously on its underside. "Stop it!" said Lady Fisher sternly. "That's an antique." Lord Fisher took the little horse from her and began painstakingly to clean out its half-crown-sized hoof. If you are accustomed to ordinary horses, the presence of a Falabella makes you feel fifteen feet tall: they look like big horses, act like horses, smell like horses, yet barely come up to your hip pocket. Physiologically, they are normal, although they have two fewer vertebrae and ribs than others, and a remarkable lifespan— they often live to fifty and breed at thirty. The only allowances made for them at Kilverstone are those of warmth and careful

feeding made for all the exotic animals in the Fishers' Latin-American wildlife park.

It must be admitted that until a photographer wheedles them into it, the Fishers don't usually invite the little horses indoors. "They occasionally break out," says Lady Fisher, "and follow someone in to raid the kitchen." Mainly, they are a star attraction of the outdoor park, with the duties of breeding, jumping—riderless, of course—over miniature showjumps in the paddock, and occasionally pulling carriages.

"I'd love to see a team of the spotted Appaloosian ones in harness with a carriage, but we've never had time," says Lady Fisher. "They enjoy pulling. But they like jumping most, and they're great showmen. One of the tiniest is Pandora—you have to sit down to groom her, and she gets on your knee—and the first time she jumped she knocked something with her nose, and everyone in the crowd laughed. So she went round flopping all the rest of the bars off, to get more applause." They do a lot of showbiz work away from home, too. Why not, when you can travel with four of them in comfort in the back of a Ford Transit van? They seem to enjoy that as well. "One of them was stood on a roulette wheel for the Little and Large Show, it was some joke about putting a pony on a bet. We put one of our little monkeys on as well," she parenthesized, losing the drift for a moment as a small horse dug her in the back. "Is there a sum of money called a monkey? There must be. Anyway, I thought the mare would hate it, so I got the grooms to pop her on a table every day beforehand and give her half a biscuit, for practice. In no time she was loving tables and refusing to get off. They really are complete characters."

The showbiz and modelling opportunities are enormous: Kilverstone was the first Falabella stud in Europe: normally the Argentinian family are unwilling to let stallions or in-foal mares leave the ranch, and the foals are extremely valuable as the ultimate prestige pet. Despite their amenable cuteness, however, the little horses behave in a refreshingly wild manner in private. "They never bite me, but they bite and kick each other," says Lady Fisher. "Usually over food and sex, their main preoccupations."

She brushes aside any suggestion that it is perverse to breed horses—the most useful of animals—down to a size where they become totally useless. "Lots of things I like are useless. Pictures, china cherubs. Falabellas are lovely for someone like me who loves horses, the look of them and the smell and their nature, but doesn't ride any longer. I'm too stiff, you see. But these horses just suit me, you don't have to exercise them, you can take them for a walk on a lead. And they're good lawnmowers, the only kind that I can start, anyway." Certainly, they are a prime attraction. The public like

miniature horses; and on one great day, the Queen turned out to like them, too.

"We took some to the Rare Breeds show at Windsor, and the horses were put in wonderful stables, with such deep bedding they were almost floating in it, just their noses sticking out. They were pigging themselves eating it. When the Queen came and spent ten minutes with us, she was quite worried that they shouldn't be stuffing so much, but she loved them, in fact there's a photograph of her giving the thumbs up sign to the horses—the only time I've seen the Queen give such a gesture in public!"

The sequel to this royal patronage came when the local RAF base started flying its jets low over Kilverstone on exercises, frightening Menelik, the prized Appaloosian stallion, so much that he "nearly leapt over his ha-ha into the bison paddock". Lord Fisher rang and complained, and was told haughtily that the noisy jets were going about Her Majesty's business. When he riposted that Her Majesty was a personal friend of Menelik's herd, he got a distinct sense of not being believed.

Weeks later, they heard indirectly that the senior officer in question was in conversation with the Queen, and said, "Put up a bit of a black the other day, ma'am, flew low over Kilverstone."

To which his sovereign replied, "What! That's the home of the Falabella horses! I hope you didn't disturb them!" Since then, the jets take another route.

In the hall, Lady Fisher slipped off her little fillies' neat coats—"Made by the people who make bodywarmers for lifeboatmen." Pale Argentina, chestnut Petra and little grey Karla milled around, snapping at the dried flowers and pawing the carpet.

Their groom looked on affectionately. "It's like working with normal horses, but they don't hurt so much when they step on you."

"Oh yes, they do," said Lady Fisher. "It's like someone in a stiletto heel standing on your foot." Jenny Wren the chihuahua hurled herself around in paroxysms of excitement. "Small monkeys, miniature donkeys, horses, dogs ... why do I like miniature things?" muses Lady Fisher, smoothing a mane. "Suppose because I'm not miniature myself. I'm quite ordinary. I've had children, so it can't be anything odd about me, substitute children or anything." Her husband finished cleaning Argentina's little foot with his penknife and straightened up with a groan. His wife sympathized.

"When we first started the herd ten years ago, we looked for a very small blacksmith to trim their feet. I found a tiny one, but even he said that it was too far to bend down, and he never came again. Now we have the tallest blacksmith in East Anglia, but he seems to manage. He's an uncomplaining man."

THE FIRST PONY:

Matthew Fligg and Noddy

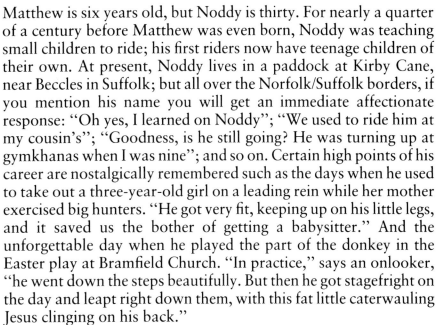

Matthew is six years old, but Noddy is thirty. For nearly a quarter of a century before Matthew was even born, Noddy was teaching small children to ride; his first riders now have teenage children of their own. At present, Noddy lives in a paddock at Kirby Cane, near Beccles in Suffolk; but all over the Norfolk/Suffolk borders, if you mention his name you will get an immediate affectionate response: "Oh yes, I learned on Noddy"; "We used to ride him at my cousin's"; "Goodness, is he still going? He was turning up at gymkhanas when I was nine"; and so on. Certain high points of his career are nostalgically remembered such as the days when he used to take out a three-year-old girl on a leading rein while her mother exercised big hunters. "He got very fit, keeping up on his little legs, and it saved us the bother of getting a babysitter." And the unforgettable day when he played the part of the donkey in the Easter play at Bramfield Church. "In practice," says an onlooker, "he went down the steps beautifully. But then he got stagefright on the day and leapt right down them, with this fat little caterwauling Jesus clinging on his back."

In all his thirty years, Noddy has never changed hands for money, except when he was an ugly six-month-old foal living in someone's potting shed, and was first spotted by the Hon. Mrs Rous of Dennington Hall. He was ridden by the Rous children; each in turn outgrew him and passed him on to younger friends; recently, since his owner's death, he has been under the wardship of a local riding teacher, Rose Hart. She lends him out to kind and careful families with small children. He lives on grass and hay, and has never been ill in his life. He may not be a Grand National winner, but in his way, in his rare and happy combination of the right stature and the right nature, Noddy is just as singular a creature. "Ponies like that really are as rare as hens' teeth," Rose

Hart says. "Normally, a very small pony like a pure-bred Shetland is quite difficult and stubborn, so they're not all that suitable for a little child in spite of the size. But Noddy, though he's tiny, isn't pure Shetland—nobody knows what his other half is, could be anything." The mystery parent bequeathed Noddy a big, rather ugly head to replace the fine Shetland one, and an angelically quiet temperament. However small you are, you can sit on his back and he will spring no surprises; you can take ten minutes trying to mount him by yourself, ending up back to front, and through it all Noddy will stand still, meditating, on his solid hairy legs. And if you lose a stirrup and slither off, it isn't far to fall.

So Matthew Fligg, son of a print-worker, is Noddy's current jockey, and bumps up and down the thistly field with the nonchalant confidence of four years' practice. "And I tell him jokes, sometimes," he says, whispering in a hairy ear while his mother tacks up for him. "Good old Noddy."

Matthew, his mother says, has even been hunting. "He jumps the little ditches. And he goes to Pony Club."

"I've got rosettes," says Matthew.

"Well, all the children who've had Noddy have got rosettes," qualifies his mother. "He knows what to do, you see." Last year, Rose offered Matthew a bigger pony, but he wasn't ready to change; it is a not uncommon problem. For who would gladly part with Noddy? From his greying forelock to his woolly hindquarters, he represents utter security, steerability, and stoppability. "Matthew," says his mother, "often trots around screaming his head off, and I think he's out of control and frightened, but it turns out he's loving every minute of it." Noddy doesn't mind the squeals. He's heard every noise a six-year-old can make, in his time.

Catching Noddy is no problem. The moment you step into the field he shares with Herbie the chestnut pony, the pair of them get so close to you that the problem is getting your arms far enough from your body to lift the bridle to the willing old mouth. Persuading Noddy and Herbie to separate by more than a couple of paces is more difficult. We eventually took some stirring pictures of Matthew trotting briskly towards the camera on his own, by the simple expedient of holding Herbie just behind Kit, then leading an unwilling but politely co-operative Noddy to the far end of the field to release him like a homing pigeon to find his friend. "I'm afraid Noddy's a leading-rein pony, really, these days," apologizes Mrs Fligg. "He'll trot and canter, if you lead him, but he won't do much at all otherwise. But that's what you want with very small children, isn't it?"

It is what Matthew wants, for the moment. Clinging to the pommel of the ancient saddle, he bumps towards us, and slides off to give Noddy another cuddle. "I know what this bit's called, I can remember," he informs us. "Forelock. That's his forelock." You learn things about horses when you've got Noddy in your back garden: the nice things about them, anyway.

THE POLICE HORSE:

PC Poole and Pickwick

You might think, churlishly, that there is nothing particularly special about a police horse. But if you talk to any long-serving mounted officer he, or she, will tell you that this may be so, but that a "special" horse is the last thing a police officer needs. A courageous horse, yes; a trustworthy one, certainly; but that high-bred "specialness" that gives the Arab its fire or the thoroughbred its speed has no place in a stable of police horses. No temperament is encouraged here, no delicate ways, no rolling eyes behind the perspex blinkers or sulkily flared nostrils. The Greater Manchester Police Mounted Division has forty of what it insists are "ordinary" horses, mostly bought from Ireland, with which they have controlled everything from crowds at Beatles concerts to over-excited and violent Liverpool football fans, to downright hostile striking miners.

Yet, surprisingly, in twenty-seven years, Chief Inspector Norman Brown claims, "There has been no serious injury to a horse. In fact, they seem to get more cuts and bruises in the stables than they ever do when they're on the job." He paused and smiled. "You've got to think of them as fifteen hundredweight, delicately poised on four steel shoes. They can get out of the way fairly quickly." They are born survivors, because they have to be. And as survivors go, Pickwick and his rider, Constable Tony Poole, have not done badly. Theirs is one of the longest partnerships in any British police force, and they're not tired of one another yet.

"Pickwick's one of our lighter horses," says PC Poole, beginning his description with cautious conventionality. "Fit as a fiddle." But then he admits the horse's more wayward charms. "Well, he can be a rum lad. He'll bugger off if you don't keep hold of him, won't you, old lad?" Pickwick gets a hefty slap across his rump from the

long arm of the law. "I've been offered younger horses but I'd never swap him. Ours is the longest partnership in the Section and as far as I'm concerned, it's a privilege to be allowed to stay with him." Like all mounted officers, Tony Poole did his time on the beat and in the patrol cars before ever getting near a horse. No horse-mad lad is ever allowed to sign up directly for the mounted section; they are carefully chosen from volunteers who already have a wide-ranging experience of police work. Quite often, the choice does not rely on their riding experience, either. "We used to teach new riders from the Cavalry Manual. The military style of riding," says CI Norman Brown. "A very intensive course."

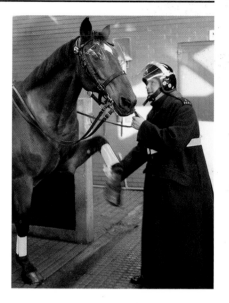

PC Poole nods, and remembers being on the receiving end. "Lots of surgical spirit needed on the backside every night."

I asked, casually, what the next day's work might hold in store for Pickwick and PC Poole? "Nothing special," said the constable. "There's a couple of football matches, a hunt meet where we're expecting a bit of trouble, and there's an El Al flight to keep an eye on." Of course, compared with many of the situations that Pickwick has faced, these are all easy meat indeed. The miners' strike, bitter and divisive, often violent, which disfigured the year 1984 in Britain was a hard time for police horses and their riders.

"We were on the Orgreave Coking Plant job. It was funny really, we'd be having a game of football with the pickets, and then the next thing you knew, you'd be facing the same blokes, and they'd be throwing hairy petrol bombs at you. They once set fire to a Portakabin, didn't they?"

He turns to CI Brown, who nods, "And rolled it down the hill at us."

"How did Pickwick take it?" I asked in a concerned, not to say appalled, way, remembering the fear most horses have of fire.

"Oh, he just stepped out of the way," said PC Poole unconcernedly. "He wasn't too bothered."

"It was all a bit of a mess," adds the Chief Inspector. "They had two Range Rovers driving round in circles trying to sort it out. The Range Rovers eventually collided, and then we all had to go in. We had it sorted in ten minutes." There were fifteen hundred pickets, and twelve horses. CI Brown leaned back, remembering it with the satisfaction of a general who had seen off a superior enemy with his equine armoury.

But to think of all mounted police work as confrontation would be wrong. The point about horses is not only their strength and height and agility, but that fortunate quality they have of making people, on the whole, feel well-disposed towards them. And in traditional unarmed British policing, the goodwill of the public is central to the job.

"We'll go into any rough area," says PC Poole, "and there's an instant rapport. It's unlike the reaction you get in a police car. It's the most rewarding part of the job really. You can meet up with the biggest villain: he won't run a mile at the sight of you, he'll bring his kiddy out to give a sweet to the horse instead. And when you're in the middle of a football crowd, you can have a joke with them. You say: 'What a wally that United player was!' And then you've got them where you want them. We're eight feet off the ground; we can see and be seen and that's a great advantage."

If pressed very hard, PC Tony Poole will admit to one weakness in his old friend Pickwick. "I must admit, I have a bit of trouble

with him at kick-off time. You see, he knows when the whistle goes, he hears it and then he reckons his job is done and he wants to be back in his stable. If the crowd's not all inside the ground by then, I've got problems."

Unkindly, I raised the spectre that haunts all mounted officers, or at least the ones who love their work almost as much as their horses: the notion of having to return to the cars again. Tony Poole goes quiet. "I don't think about it. I really try not to think about it." And Pickwick? He won't last for ever on the beat, will he? "I don't know about that. At the moment, he's pushing twenty and he's doing the work of a four-year-old. There's no stopping him."

THE DRESSAGE HORSE:

Jennie Loriston-Clarke and Dutch Courage

Dutch Courage is a solid dark-brown stallion with a friendly eye and noticeably muscular legs. He is not tall, only 16.1, which comes as rather a shock when you have seen him in the arena, carrying Jennie Loriston-Clarke through the curious skimming, floating, graceful movements of top-class dressage. In the ring, he looks enormous and formidably powerful, betraying his Gelderlander carriage-horse ancestry. "Well, people do think he's bigger," says his owner affectionately. "He has such presence and authority."

Between them, Jennie Loriston-Clarke and Dutch Courage have displayed presence, authority and skill in such measure that they can be credited with bringing the sport into real prominence in Britain, for the first time. For many years, dressage was considered a bit of a bore by the public, and a slightly irritating inconvenience to three-day event riders who would rather be hurtling over fences than trying to persuade their superfit, flighty horses to trot on the spot. In mainland northern Europe dressage was important and respected; in Britain, it remained more of an eccentric minority pursuit. But respect is growing for it here since Jennie Loriston-Clarke won a bronze medal in the World Championships in 1978, and a team of younger riders came home from Europe with a silver medal in 1986. Jennie's daughter, Ann, was in the team, riding Dutch Courage's son, Dutch Bid. As she remarks proudly, "We bred the horse *and* the rider." Public appreciation is also growing, not least thanks to Jennie's enthusiasm for freestyle dressage performed to music. After all, only a horseman can really appreciate the grace and difficulty of the movements themselves, but anyone can enjoy the balletic quality of a horse that does the same movements to *Edelweiss* or selections from *Aïda*.

Jennie has ridden in cross-country events, jumped, point-to-

pointed and done a bit of everything; but from the moment in her childhood when she saw Madame Hartel, the Danish silver medallist, she hankered for dressage. "I never was the bravest of riders, I didn't like having to push a horse, but neither do I like runaways; I always like to be properly in control, yet still have that thoroughbred sharpness and intelligence and quickness to work with. When I had children, and didn't want to go over tall fences any more, it was the logical thing to do." It was also logical for another, deeper reason: Jennie Loriston-Clarke is that rare thing, a natural animal trainer.

"It's always fascinated me. That rapport between anyone and their animal—whatever the species. There was a chap at Bertram Mills's circus called Kerr, who wrote a book called *No Bars Between*, he just had a way of touching an animal and relaxing it. I like to get a rapport; once a horse understands what you want, he's very pleased to do it. I could just go on training and breeding and riding horses for ever; it is so fascinating to ride the young horse when you've ridden the parent, and understand how traits are coming through, and learn not to make the same mistakes you made with the parent." Despite the criticism of dressage by some riders as pointless and unnatural, Jennie finds the opposite. "Oh, they are all natural movements. I had a Welsh cob who used to do the *piaffe* [the standing trot] by himself in his stable, just out of excitement. And horses will sometimes put in a change of leg, just to please you, when you don't ask for it. And it is very satisfying both for you and for the horse when the horse is carrying itself correctly; everything is easier when it is in the correct balance. Of course, dressage can be terribly boring for a horse, day-in-day-out training—so I vary it carefully." As for the moments in the ring, she enjoys them, but not overwhelmingly, not being a particular show-off by nature. "Riding is a very personal satisfaction; but it's just so beautiful, especially dressage to music, that the audience do love it. That's good."

All these threads come together in the complacent, good-natured, shiningly dark and eminently balanced figure of Dutch Courage, now standing at stud at Jennie's Catherston Stud in the New Forest. She found him in Holland when he was three. "I kept going back to him, after I'd seen just his nose and eyes peering over a very high door in this stable. I thought he looked quality. The others were too heavy. When they trotted him up the road for me in a snowstorm, I liked his looks and shape and head and eye; he looked bold, not a chicken. A horse that wanted to go places." He was, however, distinctly wild, hence his name: "I thought I'd need some Dutch courage to ride that!" But as a stallion, he would clearly earn his keep whatever his riding qualities.

And as it turned out, both his riding qualities and his stallion performance have been brilliant. He has occasionally combined the two, doing a day's dressage, covering a mare the next day, and back in the ring on the third. In training, "He took to everything like a duck to water. At six, he was off to Aachen and Fontainebleau. He's a horse who listens to what you say, and will always come to you, and try to please you. I just say, 'Hello, Bill', and up he walks." Why Bill? "Well, a childhood joke. My brother was always Bill and I was Fred, when we played cops and robbers. When Dutch Courage came he had that same cheeky look in his eye, so I called him Bill."

In the stud stables Bill's foals and ex-foals stand quietly in the winter dusk. Elegant, fine-lined Dutch Gold, Dutch Bid who helped to win a silver medal, Dambuster, and nervy young three-year-old Dazzle, all breathe clouds of steam into the cold air. Dutch Courage himself, merry-eyed and nimble, solidly graceful, comes across his stall to nuzzle his mistress gently for a carrot.

THE PLOUGH HORSES:

Cheryl and Roger Clark's Suffolks

Across the hard, bare, winter earth three horses plod, abreast. Ahead of them lies stony, flat, exhausted land; behind them a leaping loamy furrow of rich brown clods, alive with the promise of a new crop. There are few sights so satisfying as a horsedrawn plough at work.

Behind these three horses, as they move slowly across the south Suffolk landscape, walks a lonely figure. It could be Roger Clark, or it could be Cheryl his wife. Together they run Weylands Farm as equals, and they run it entirely with horses. They plough and cart and even spray the fields without ever hearing the sound of roaring tractors, but only the quiet, deliberate tread of their seven working Suffolk Punches. The horses pull behind them an assortment of ancient farm machinery, which looks like scrap, but works to perfection. For instance, Roger in our picture is using a two-bladed plough fitted with a little hopper of seed beans and a wheel to release the seed into the furrow. The cleverness of the old device even attracts envious glances from some mechanized farmers. With a tractor, you often go over the same ground twice, first ploughing and sowing, then covering the seed. With this Edwardian machine and three willing horses, Roger can nonchalantly plough one furrow and sow it, while simultaneously the second blade throws earth neatly over the last lot of beans, and so forth, up and down the field.

The Clarks do not farm with horses for sentimental reasons. "We couldn't afford to farm at all without the horses. Have you seen contractors' rates these days?" Occasionally, working a farm entirely by horse has its very real ergonomic and economic perks. Inter-row cultivation is uniquely possible with a delicate-stepping horse which won't crush the crop, and several horses' strength makes it possible to lift even potatoes from waterlogged land. One wet summer week Roger and Cheryl were the only people in Suffolk to get any potatoes out of the ground; they paid half their year's farm rent off a few acres' profit.

The three horses, Toby and Rupert and Thomas, walk or stand or turn obediently. At each turn, the ploughman pauses to set the plough, adjust some blade, or twitch at the orange baler-twine which holds various arcane bits and pieces in place. "Only thing is, don't forget to fill your hopper before each time. Nothing worse than getting to the other end and finding you've sowed nothing." Hot with walking, he hangs his coat on Toby's collar, and sets off again, his little dog following. The three heads bob in syncopation as the horses move off.

It would be easy, but utterly wrong, to assume that because the Clarks farm with horses, they are part of a deliberate revival or intellectual whole-earth movement. Roger, young as he is, is a genuine inheritor of an unbroken tradition, for Suffolk is a county which has always held pockets of strong resistance to change. "Early on, I never knew anything but horses. Up to 1972, remember, they were carting all the refuse over in Saxmundham with horses. Then I worked over at Coulson's at Long Melford, and he still had six working."

To continue working with horses, Roger trained as a farrier. His courtship of Cheryl, twenty years ago, was not smooth: "Her father thought, and still thinks, that I'm a gypsy." But as soon as she reached twenty-one, they defiantly married. Instead of the traditional elopement of going off to Gretna Green to be married by a blacksmith, Cheryl carried out her own variation on the theme: she married and *became* a blacksmith. She, as well as Roger, is a qualified farrier. "When we first started out, things were at an all-time low ebb in horses. Foot and mouth meant we couldn't shoe for a whole year. We used to exercise people's point-to-pointers at seven and six an hour." Cheryl carried on shoeing, virtually full-time, for nearly ten years; although today, with the little farm to manage as well, Roger does the shoeing and she concentrates on her particular forte, breaking heavy horses to harness.

It is no job for a coward. Shire horses are being bred today for the showring rather than the plough, and come to Cheryl often after two years of being shown off "in hand", spoilt and unworked. "Wicked, some of them. What I do is make them fight theirselves, instead of me. That way they're bound to give up, and learn to respect what I say, which they all do in the end." She uses ancient, cunning devices: hobbles and straps; ties which make a horse uncomfortable if it lies down, or unable to rear without toppling. "In the end, they all take notice."

"Someone once asked me," says Roger, "When are you master of a horse? Not when you say whoa, and it stops. You're master, he said, when it's done a day's work, and it's got one foot in its stable and sees its feed, and *then* you say whoa, and it stops."

"But I don't like horses without a bit of spirit," qualifies Cheryl. "I like a horse that holds hisself up, that's got presence."

The couple go, with mischievous enjoyment, into a dissertation on why after their beloved Suffolks they consider Ardennes heavy horses to be boring. "Lump o' meat on four stakes," says Roger. "You dare to write that, and see what they say." Neither do they have much time for the growing number of Suffolks which are only used in shows, and don't do proper work. "We could never have anything around that wasn't doing anything. All our horses that win the shows"—and they do, consistently—"work on the farm, hard. There's a different type of fitness you see in a horse that works in harness. Some of the Suffolks you see now, they win prizes when they're soft, fat, straight off the meadow. They look all right, if you don't know what a really fit horse looks like; but put them to a plough and they'd melt like snow."

The Clarks don't breed: "We'd rather buy. You get what you want, when you buy. What we look for each time is a big upstanding horse, a gelding, one that gets his height through his depth of heart, not his length of leg." Thomas and Toby and Rupert, the day's ploughing team, exemplify the solid ancient working breed of Suffolks that Roger and Cheryl love. "They're not soft. They're not always quiet, either. Thomas and Toby can play up. Reason they don't play up right now is they're well under the thumb."

But even Cheryl, passionate though she is about the horses, doesn't like to talk of favourites. "For instance, I like ploughing best with Rupert and Courtier, but that's just because they plough the way I like to plough."

Roger tries to explain: "We don't like a horse so much for the way he is, as for the things he does."

Back in the top field, the brass glints on the horses' brows in the late winter sunlight. Across the pale field they move, leaving a glistening arrow-straight trace of dark earth behind them. Three Suffolk Punches, strong as Samson and patient as Job, stepping across the land and making it new again.

THE RETIRED RACEHORSE:

Lord Oaksey and Tuscan Prince

John Oaksey, best known amateur jockey of his time, has ridden in eleven Grand Nationals. He has been first past the winning post two hundred times. If you did not know it, you would guess he was a jockey from the way he strides across the lawn of his Wiltshire farmhouse. Surely it cannot be rude to refer to a jockey as "bandy-legged". It is as much an honourable mark of his trade as a flattened thumb to a joiner; anyway, it must be said that Oaksey walks very much like a jockey.

We were making our way to the paddock at the end of the lawn where lives Tuscan Prince, a retired racehorse. He is luckier than some. What usually becomes of old racehorses is never quite certain. Very few simply fade away. Some youngsters are stretched physically beyond their years in pursuit of victory, and are played-out when they should really be coming into their prime, injured and crippled to the point that they have to be shot. Others are bred from such fiery and spirited lines that only a professional rider can hope to hold them; they often end up shot, too. A few have a satisfactory afterlife as hunters. "Yes, I suppose it's the lucky ones who get turned out," says Oaksey. "Many of them are certainly put down. But when this old lad got to thirteen, they asked me whether I would like him. I thought he would make a first-class hunter, so I took him." It sounds cool, and calculating. But when Lord Oaksey begins to remember the glorious victories that were won astride "Tuscy", then it becomes clear that this is more than a convenient arrangement, and that it was never a typically shallow passing relationship between a jockey and his ride. "I first rode him in an amateur race at Sandown. 7 January 1972. We won by ten lengths! He was a brilliant jumper; I rode him in twenty-two races and won five of them. And do you know, there is no record of a fall. That's quite remarkable. He really was a superlative jumper. When

a horse has carried you that far without falling, you get very fond of him. He's given me enormous fun."

Tuscy makes his way towards us. It is no longer the spirited stride that might have caught a punter's eye in the collecting ring. "He's a bit arthritic in his hind legs, you know," says Oaksey, "we can't shoe him all round now. You just can't lift his legs high enough." He stares long and hard at the old horse, noting his condition, and a smile breaks across his face. "He was a wonderful ride. Quite a pull for a girl, but a wonderful ride. The children ride him now and again, but without a saddle."

We return to the house, and to Lord Oaksey's study, where he delves into his collection of the form books: the bibles of the horseracing world where glorious victories jostle alongside ignominious defeats. Oaksey thumbs through them with an expert's eye—he is racing correspondent of the *Daily Telegraph* and learned columnist of the *Horse and Hound* magazine. "I was only ever an amateur. I suppose in 1957 or '58, you could say I caught fire briefly. I've won the Whitbread Gold Cup, and the Hennessy Gold Cup." He has always earned his living as a journalist, what he disparagingly calls "a hack writer. Originally, I was supposed to be a lawyer. My father had presided over the Nuremberg trials. But he was very good when I told him I'd got a job as second racing correspondent on the *Telegraph*. I thought it was just marvellous, because I actually got paid to go racing." He delves deeper into the form books, dusty ones now, looking for Tuscy's story. "He was born in 1970 . . . trained by the great Tom Draper. He trained Arkle, you know! I wonder if Tuscy and Arkle could have been in the stable at the same time?" This question sends him deeper into the small print for a while, but regretfully he decides in the end that they probably weren't. Outside, in the paddock, Tuscy pauses for a moment from his grazing, and looks up at us through the study window, then drops his old head again, contentedly. Lord Oaksey gives him a fond glance.

"He's quite eccentric, you know. When we bring him back to his box at night, he will never walk straight in. He stands and freezes as if he had seen a ghost. He's very greedy too. And he shouts a lot. He likes to make an exhibition of himself." Oaksey looks out, and spots Tuscy looking in again. "If I had any criticism of him in our racing days, it would be that he tended to stop after he'd jumped the last fence. He's very much a horse that you have to get on your side. If he were a human being, I would say that he wouldn't be all that brave. But a great charmer. Suave, you might say." Oaksey pauses for thought. "He'd be a suave old clubman." He laughs. "Do you know, the last time he was ridden he ran away with my daily's daughter. He's never ever run off before, old Tuscy." One more record, one more small victory, for Tuscan Prince. Not one destined for the form books, though. Lord Oaksey shuts them, and puts them back on the shelf, full of tributes to old times. And old horses. Outside, Tuscy ambles off to a fresh patch of grass.

THE SHOW-PONY:

Jemima Goldsmith and Moorhall Elegance

"Ellie," says Jemima Goldsmith happily, "can be quite lazy. But she's absolutely sweet. I'd put a two-year-old on her and send her into the showring, and Ellie would look after her. She's just a hundred per cent safe. You need to make her step out, though, or she'd just poodle along peacefully and not bother with anything."

Moorhall Elegance, it is quite clear, is not cut out to be one of those sparky, rowdy gymkhana ponies on which Pony Club kids gallop through energetic relay races or leap over fences. Ellie, sweet, gentle, dappled creature, is a top show-pony whose job is to look utterly perfect in the ring, and be judged on her elegant physique, pretty paces and ladylike behaviour. On her back, Jemima too must look immaculate.

"You have to be the right size for the pony, because if you're too tall above its back, or too fat, you look ghastly. You have to have your hair-ribbon matching the browband on the bridle, your jodhpurs two sizes too small so they don't wrinkle, and your jodhpur boots so polished there isn't a speck on them. Sometimes I have to be given a piggyback to the edge of the ring so I don't get them dirty." Thus, groomed to a hair, pony and rider go through their paces, walking and trotting and cantering past the critical eyes of the judges and under the equally critical, and occasionally hostile, eyes of their peers and attendant mothers. "In the ring, you really have to keep your concentration. I try desperately hard to do everything right and not let Ellie down, because she's so brilliant. It's competitive all right; in the group ride, people will cut you up

and try and get in front of you when you're doing your flashy trot, so the judges don't see." She smiles reminiscently. "My friend Kelly and I have plots about that sort of thing. It's very intense, and I'm exhausted, afterwards. But I really love the shows, there's such a buzz in it. I've got definite faults: I don't sit up, or look up, properly. My legs are all right, though." Jemima sounds as absorbed and self-critical as an adult competitor for a moment, then suddenly giggles like the thirteen-year-old schoolgirl she is. "I love it. But my brother Zack gave it up. He can't bear going to shows, he always says, 'Oh, no, we don't have to see Jemima riding again, yuk.' And my little brother, who's seven, really hates all the dressing up, says its poofy. They only like coming to shows if there's a funfair."

Showing is a curious sort of competition, refined, some say, to the point of absurdity. As Jemima says with enthusiasm: "You just have to get out there and *prove* that your pony is the prettiest." But in this rarefied world Jemima Goldsmith and Ellie have become stars. They won a clutch of county shows in their first season together, qualified for the Horse of the Year Show at Wembley, and—"the greatest triumph"—won the Tower McCall Classic at Peterborough, the most prestigious show of all. It is a world where money counts—money to buy the right pony, to wear the right clothes, to afford the necessary transport to get to distant shows in Cumbria or Cornwall—so it is lucky for Jemima that her father happens to be the millionaire financier Sir James Goldsmith. However, without a certain dedication, even the most pampered rider couldn't win at the top level. Jemima and Ellie have a punishing training schedule to keep themselves immaculate for the ring. "There's a lot of work, there really is. Almost every weekend I have a show, in summer; I do jumping on my other pony, Moidy, in the winter; I practise three or four times a week, and it's an hour's drive after school to get to the Ramsays at Finchampstead where they 'produce' my ponies. I don't always feel like going, but I do. And the lessons aren't all fun, they're very tough, and they can be boring."

Sometimes it is the parents—usually the mothers—who are the most dedicated to winning. Pony-show mothers are notorious for pushing their daughters ruthlessly, and for harassing the judges. One seasoned judge expressed to me the view that "It ought to be a qualification that every child in showing classes should be an orphan with no relatives whatsoever." Jemima admits that "Some people do, er, Not Very Nice Things to get ahead." This does not, she adds firmly, apply to her own mother, Lady Annabel: "She isn't pushy, honestly. She just gets annoyed if the pony does well and I let it down, that's all, and I get upset myself if that happens. She

encouraged me to ride, and I'm really really glad she did."

Riding began, for Jemima, when she was eight or nine. She was a fast learner but not, she admits engagingly, particularly brave. "I don't think I'll ever have the bottle to be a showjumper or a cross-country rider. I'd like to show hacks next, and do more dressage." Her first pony was a broken-winded mare called April "who used to bolt with me"; then Patrick, who was "meant to jump, but didn't"; then Speedy, who was the wrong size "and I hadn't a clue how to ride him"; then Velvet who came on Christmas morning with a big sash round her, as a present, and who was voted "brilliant". She won't hear a word against any of them, loves them all dearly and still owns several of them. Ellie, however, is special.

"Mum saw her, and thought she was the most beautiful thing in the world. She'd come third at Wembley with Pippa Nichol, and she was out of the same stallion as Velvet is, Wingrove Minkino. We'd tried her, but Mum didn't tell me until she'd actually bought Ellie. She was just so perfect." In the ring, Ellie needs, above all, skilled impulsion from her rider, because of her tendency to "plodge along". Whereas Velvet needs riding for half an hour beforehand to "take the edge off her", five minutes on Ellie is enough if you don't want to flatten her out entirely. "You need a bit of spark in them in the ring, because they look better."

The show circuit keeps Jemima utterly rapt and involved. "Everything works up to Wembley, and it's just so exciting; then afterwards you're really mourning, for a couple of weeks, it's all so flat." Her mother goes to shows with her, funfair-seeking sons in tow, and her father comes occasionally, "Though I think really he puts up with it more than liking it. He doesn't like riding making me late for lunch, for instance. But we always ring him up wherever he is if I have a major triumph."

Like English parents through many generations, the Goldsmiths have the satisfaction of knowing that their daughter has an absorbing, dedicated interest to steer her safely clear of the rockier coasts of adolescence. Jemima is no fool, and puts it quite clearly. "A lot of people in our class just go in for balls and things, and spend masses of money on new clothes and fashions and all that. I'm really lucky. I've got a hobby, they don't know what to do with themselves. I'm not all that keen on clothes and dances and things; I can't think what I'd do if I didn't ride. I can't imagine ever giving it up."

The only cloud on the horizon is that Ellie and Jemima will soon be parted. "She's 13.2. I knew when I got her that I'd only got a couple of years until I outgrew her. Oh, I do wish she'd sprout up suddenly, and grow with me! We'll have to sell her, unless we put her in foal. But we won't sell her to just any old person. Never!"

THE APPLEBY FAIR DEAL:

Joe Wilson and Brighteyes

Joe Wilson is fourteen. His father, Joe senior, is a horse-dealer in Kent, and young Joe has no doubt whatever that he will follow him into the trade. He is, rather reluctantly, still at school, but would not dream of being there during that heady week in June when dealers from all over Britain gather on a Cumbrian hillside for Appleby Fair. The horses come in every kind of box and lorry, or some local ones on their own legs; from early morning onwards the owners paddle them around in the River Eden, casually cleaning the mud off in the pebbly shallows. The sight of a dozen horses, half of them still harnessed to exercise-carts, wandering nonchalantly around under the town bridge draws a crowd of spectators. The cosy little town, with its decorous tourist shops and old-fashioned pubs, wears an air of mingled apprehension and excitement; it has been invaded again, and there is nothing to be done about it.

Appleby Fair is a traditional gypsy gathering, run by the gypsies themselves; but among the showmanship and furtive betting of the travellers' high-speed trotting races, thousands of pounds' worth of solid transactions in horseflesh are made. To attract attention to their horses, the dealers have them ridden, or trotted with a cart, at breakneck speed up and down a crowded road just outside the town. Half-broken young horses buck and sweat and jib, break into a gallop, are reined up sharp, nudge and prance and dodge one another's flying kicks. Miraculously, nobody seems to get hurt. On the grass verge alongside, dozens more horses are tethered, bewildered foals huddling desperately up to their mothers, itchy yearlings throwing their heads angrily up against rope halters. Farriers work from ancient vans, harness of all types, both new and dilapidated, is sold from the sides of wagons, and here and there the back of a lorry will open to reveal an array of suspiciously cheap cushions, or tasselled curtain-pulls. The crowd surges

around, parting sharply every few minutes to let through a foam-
ing, clattering horse and rider at full speed.

Young Joe's job at Appleby is to ride up and down in a furious
manner aboard whatever his father is trying to sell: in this case
Brighteyes, a six-year-old piebald mare. "Worth eight hundred,"
Joe says briefly. Brighteyes puffs, drooping her strong neck after
the exertion of the past half-hour. "Eight hundred," says Joe
hopefully, again. "Interested?" He has been riding horses, broken
and unbroken, ever since he could walk, and fallen off "hundreds
of times". Nobody taught him, he says; "lessons" are not part of
his world view. On horseback, his style is not exactly what you
might call classic Pony Club. "You gets on, stay on the best you
can. That's what." He would certainly never use a saddle. "Suppose one takes off with us, you falls off, you'd get caught up in it
and pulled along." Brighteyes, he concedes, is a "good 'orse"; but
he has no sentimental attachment for her or for any other, and
indeed he can't remember ever feeling any particular liking, or
dislike, for any individual horse. After some thought, he con-
cluded: "I likes the ones that earn the money!" Joe has made real

deals, he says, all by himself. "Most sale I made was three thousand."

He soon grows restless with talking; the high drama of Appleby Fair is too brief to waste in conversation. Anyway, with every passing minute potential buyers might be escaping without having had their chance to see Brighteyes hurtling back along the road with Joe balanced on her sweating back. So, "I'll get off again." One last question: why does he wear his cap backwards? "So it stay on, o'course," he says scornfully, and accelerates Brighteyes into the heart of the crowd, shouting "Hoy!"

"Aye," says an elderly local dealer, eyeing up boy and horse. "No' a bad pony." What about the boy? Good at the job? "Keeps it going, anyway." And Joe rattles off, past dapple-greys and Appaloosas, cobs and Shetlands, stallions and shaky foals; past festoons of harness, flicking whips, flailing tails, and milling spectators. And on the sidelines the dealers wink and nod, tap their noses, slap solid beer-guts, and sometimes carefully pull out thousands of pounds, in notes, from the depths of greasy pockets.

THE KEY TO FREEDOM:

Jackie Croome and Checkmate

Jackie Croome is a friendly, delicately pretty redhead of twenty-five, about to be married. She is also paraplegic: eight years ago she broke her back in a fall which left her helpless from the waist down. She now sees the world from wheelchair height. This makes her one of the many victims of life's cruellest irony, that it is the young, the physically brave and fit, who suffer these accidents and lose their prized physical coherence for ever. In Jackie's case, she was a police cadet, and had the accident as she went over an assault course during her training.

A few times each week, however, she can once more move fast and surely, with all that lost athleticism, thanks to a horse. Checkmate, a cobby skewbald hunter, lends her his muscles, and raises her to his impressive height of 15.2. "He gives me freedom. That's the main thing. If you're in the middle of a field in a wheelchair, you get nowhere fast. If you're in the saddle, you can go in any direction as fast as anyone else."

The Riding for the Disabled Association has been one of the most successful initiatives for physically and mentally handicapped people in recent years. Paraplegics, spastics, amputees, Down's syndrome children, almost every kind of disabled rider can be catered for: some ride supported on either side by running helpers, and will always need them; others make startling progress. Jackie, who goes to the South Buckinghamshire group, belittles her own achievement when she cites Tony, a seventeen-year-old without hands, who rides bruising cross-country courses; Philippa, a thalidomide victim without arms who saddles her own horse with her feet, and gallops with only foot-reins for control; and countless terribly disabled or retarded children who take up the reins with joy and courage every week.

She herself took two years after her accident to pluck up the

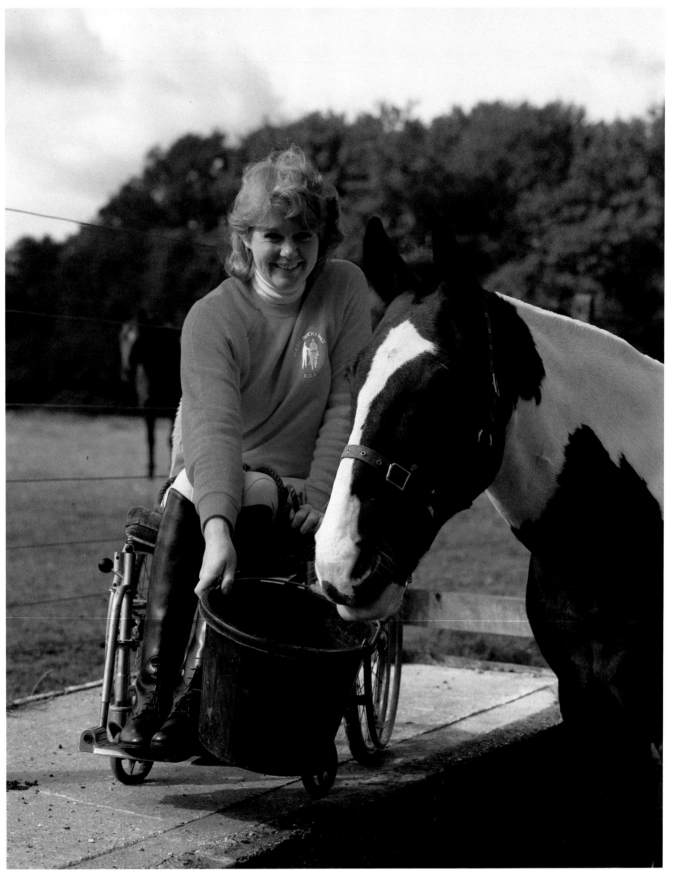

114

nerve. "I had ridden before, from when I was nine to when I was sixteen, and given it up for my 'A' levels. Actually, my favourite thing was always dressage, which is lucky because that's what I can still do now. But when I did go back to horses after the accident, I felt terrible, it was like sitting on top of a pyramid. With no feeling in my legs, I couldn't balance, I could topple in any direction. People ran alongside, with a hand on each of my legs." After a while, she gave up the helpers and learned to balance, with her feet twisted into ordinary rubber bands on each stirrup. Leg aids to the horse are out of the question, but, "That leaves my voice, hands, back and seat. I've got some control in the thigh muscles now, just these last few years; and when I do dressage I have a dressage stick as a substitute leg aid. I can ride a conventionally schooled horse; I've even ridden a young four-year-old, my greatest achievement. And in the year of practising for Sweden, I had to ride all sorts of strange horses, because that's what we'd be doing over there."

She went to Sweden in 1987 as one of the British team of six in the first equestrian world championships for the disabled. In the event, Jackie was ill and couldn't ride; but the occasion was an eye-opener. "We saw just how much you can do—the Americans were all terribly disabled, but they were tremendous. And there was a marvellous Colombian boy who'd read about it in the paper, raised money, and just came. He'd never been on a horse before, was all over the place, but we all took him to our hearts, and let him career about." International competition also gave her a curious insight into the difference between British horsemen and women and most others. "We're far more fussy and cosy with our horses. The British were always asking for more bedding, or in and out of the boxes checking things, grooming, talking, patting. None of the others could believe how close we were to the horses. Nicko, the one I practised on there, had never had a titbit before he met us. But he loved being spoilt a bit. I think British horses have more character, because we *give* them character."

The event spurred her to her next ambition: to compete in dressage against able-bodied riders. "No reason why not, at least at novice and intermediate level; I think the dressage stick would be allowed there at least." But one of the pleasures of ending the long training for Sweden was that after the event she was allowed to return to her regular mount, Checkmate.

"Oh, I had missed him. I can ride other horses, but I do like Checkmate. He's a strong horse, and bigger than most of the ones in the group—usually they don't go above 14.2, because it's a problem helping people on and off. But although I can be lifted on to him, just, he's tall and strong, and quite temperamental. He used to be known as Jaws, because he grabbed anything that passed him. But with me, he's very amenable, very gentle. Horses do change, you know; a lot of the RDA ponies really give the able-bodied grooms a hard time, but if you put a disabled child or adult on their back they're gentle as lambs. I don't know what it is: they seem to sense something."

Physically, Jackie on a horse is now much like any other competent rider on a horse. She has strong arms, reinforced by constant wheelchair propulsion, and a good seat—"I only lose my balance when they scoot sideways suddenly." Jumping is a problem, although she does low fences, simply because a paraplegic can't muster the lower body strength to rise and adjust her weight as the horse goes over the jump. "I just wouldn't have enough control to balance over a tall fence." As for stable work, she does whatever she can. "I have to groom the bottom half while Mum does the high bits." She mucks out and puts rugs on the horse's back, and feeds him, all from the wheelchair. An irritating problem of paralysis is the cold, in winter: her saddle has to have a thick wool pile cover to prevent too much cold and pressure sores.

But basically, she says, there are not too many problems. "And it

isn't the horses that cause them, it's the people. People need to know just how much to help you and not to help you. The worst thing is falling off, and seeing everyone gallop on before they turn back to get you. You just sit there not being able to do anything, not get up alone—suddenly you're different again." She is also mildly frustrated by not being able to tack up and mount and get herself out riding without depending on someone else for help; although she and Jeff, her fiancé, plan one day to keep horses of their own at home and ride out together.

"I'm not very good, though," says Jeff. "I need to learn myself. I'd like to ride out with Jackie regularly."

"Just for the freedom of it," Jackie says wistfully. "I miss it terribly when I don't ride for a while. You see, it's marvellous to look down on people for a change, instead of always talking up from a wheelchair."

THE ARMY HORSE:

Gunner Johnny Garner and Fred

A couple of years ago the King's Troop, the Royal Horse Artillery, were doing their famous musical drive when the horse ridden by the trumpeter, following behind the parade commander in a dramatic solo moment, decided he had had enough of military decorum for one day. Up he bucked, cantering and kicking around the arena to the horror of the commanding officer and the amusement of onlookers. The trumpeter was forced to concentrate on controlling the frisky animal, at the expense of his trumpeting. It was not one of the more glorious moments in the regiment's long history. Afterwards, word came down the hierarchy that the offending animal would not feature ever again in such prominence. He could go back into harness, pulling a gun-carriage in discreet anonymity, surrounded by other horses to keep him in line.

But nobody was really cross. "Not with *Fred*," says Gunner Johnny Garner. "Not Fred. He knew he could lark about, and it would all be just a laugh because, being Fred, he'd get away with it. Anyway, he'd never have played us up in harness, with a gun. It was just a laugh, because he was having a go at being the trumpeter's horse." Fred is, after all, eighteen years old, the oldest horse in his section, and something of an unofficial regimental mascot. Like the other horses of the King's Troop, he is a dark bay, a light Irish draught horse imported and trained by the RHA for their unique and spectacular ceremonial duties. His proper name is Wingate, his number 94. Apart from the Troop's annual summer holiday at the seaside with their horses, racing and rearing in the salt water for the good of their legs, Fred has stood in the same stall for ten years, under a fading plaque. He is groomed to a hair and exercised daily. But it is no wonder, says his friend Gunner Garner stoutly, that Fred gets "a bit bored. He's a horse who likes to be entertained. And he likes to entertain you, too."

It is not that a horse of the Troop has an undemanding job. Six animals pull each gun-carriage: a pair of wheelers, closest to the gun, who are the only brakes it has—half a ton of cannon must be stopped dead by their powerful push on their breechings; then two centre horses, who keep the traces up and keep pace; and two leaders, strong brave horses who do most of the hard pulling, and have to keep their nerve and discipline during terrifyingly close manoeuvres like the "scissors", when two gun teams cross one another with inches to spare at full gallop. Because no coachman sits aboard a gun to drive it, the left-hand horses, all three of them in line, are ridden, the riders holding the right-hand horses in hand. Three men and six horses have to work as a perfect, trusting team. A driver, like a horse, will begin his career in the least demanding role of centre horse; then progress to wheeler, then leader. Fred had a splendid career as a wheeler, but advancing age made him more suitable for the lead. "He's wonderful in the lead," says Johnny reverently. "Brave. It's bravery you need up there, just to go forward and really attack."

Johnny Garner is nineteen, only a year older than Fred. He began to ride as a child, chiefly to upstage his sister, but showed aptitude. After a year out of school in his father's building firm, he drifted back towards horses, grooming in a showjumping yard. The King's Troop has a reputation for taking on boys who aren't very experienced riders, but know horses a bit and have a Pony Club background of rowdy equestrian games and scrupulous horse-management and grooming. "They don't like lads from racing stables and that," says Johnny. "They think they're fly-boys. And they don't like expert riders, because it might be hard to get the militariness into them. Militariness is special riding: being able to ignore everything going on around you, cheers, bangs, all that. And to look smart. If you think about it, a showjumper doesn't have to look all that smart, just get the horse to go over fences. A military rider has to look smart, all the time."

Johnny applied, and was told loftily that he must join the Artillery and then hear whether he was selected for the Troop. "I said, if it isn't the Troop I won't join the Army," he says rather cockily. But he got in, and loves it. "Ah, a good gallop with the gunnery team from Marble Arch, through Hyde Park after a royal event . . . or that moment when you just slide your eyes sideways for a moment and see the Queen take the salute . . . there's nothing like it."

There is no written instruction anywhere which says that No. 94, Wingate, alias Fred, is Gunner Garner's special responsibility. But "ten times out of ten you'll find it's me grooming him. Well, other people do get frightened. He's got a bit of a reputation, see. When he starts throwing his head back and opening his mouth,

they move back. They don't understand Fred. It's just that he bores very easily, he needs to be played with. Look, I'll show you."

He led me down the spotless lines to Fred's stall. Johnny casually slipped off the horse's headcollar and turned him round to face us. The King's Troop usually groom their horses untied in these open stalls, young men stripped to the waist and gleaming with effort, horses gleaming darker beside them, the muscles of each rippling in harmony. They get very close, very trusting; it is unheard-of for a horse to walk off or give trouble during this morning ritual. "I could leave Fred an hour and a half and he'd still be here, untied." However, at the first touch of Johnny's brush the horse sidled and began to weave his head violently and alarmingly, teeth bared. I jumped back, and Johnny chortled and began playing games with the brush, shooshing the horse, daring him to grab it in his teeth. "See? He likes to be amused. And he likes attention, and publicity. When no one's looking at him, he begins to look like a very old horse, very tired. Give him a look, or let him hear the trumpet call for the musical drive, and he changes." Sure enough, the years rolled off Fred as he enjoyed his groom's attentions; his coat a bottomless gleam of black, soft as velvet, his eye bright. Outside, a trumpeter called stridently across the barracks and I looked at Fred, sentimentally hoping to see his old ears prick forward at the sound of the trumpet. He barely twitched an ear. "Ah no," said Johnny scornfully. "Those are only new trumpeters, practising. He knows better than to listen to them. All the horses here know all the trumpet-calls and how they should be done properly."

Every year, when the horses and men of the King's Troop go to

the seaside, Fred has an opportunity to show off all his tricks on holiday, including his famous *prima donna* moods. "Some days you could put a three-year-old on him quite safely. Some days, he'll have me off seven times in twenty minutes." But it is a happy interlude, cementing further the bond between young man and old horse. Gunner Garner would have loved to drive Fred in his wheeler days—"They all say he was brilliant"—but at present puts up with a junior centre position, watching his friend's powerful haunches ahead of him. By the time Johnny is a lead driver, Fred won't be up there any more.

"I hope he'll be retired into Civvy Street. With me." Johnny has put in a request to the veterinary officer to take on Fred for his retirement: it is a common enough thing for the old horses of the Troop to be cared for at the last by the men who once worked them. "I've got a stable and a field waiting for him at home in Derby. He'll be all right at grass. Some of these horses don't take to retirement at all, but Fred will, I think. And he's done a good job. He deserves his rest."

THE BROOD MARE:

Lady Tavistock and Mrs Moss

When Henrietta Tiarks was ten years old, her ambition was quite specific. "I wanted to have a pony of my own, a female pony so that she could have foals; and I wanted a lorry so that I could take her everywhere with me." Thirty-eight years on, she is Marchioness of Tavistock: mistress of Woburn Abbey, one of the great houses of England; and founder of the successful Bloomsbury Racing Stud. "But still," she says, "every time I get into my horsebox, I feel as if I was ten years old again. That thrill."

Even more romantic is the fact that she owes the fulfilment of her dream entirely to her one beloved, brilliant, magical brood mare, Mrs Moss. Without Mrs Moss, there would be no stud at Woburn at all, no horses or grooms, no lorries to drive along the leafy lanes. For the Tavistocks had a quite different occupation thrust upon them: Woburn itself, Lord Tavistock's ancestral home, which was cast upon their care quite unexpectedly long before they had reached a reasonable inheriting age. The house, and the family's famous and now successful efforts to make it pay for itself in the "stately home" business, was a sort of glorious albatross around their necks. It is a large and time-consuming management job in itself, and when they took over it was emphatically not in a position to support a hobby stud. When Lady Tavistock began breeding, the horses were few, cheap, and stabled far away from daily life at Woburn.

"I had been breeding horses for ten years, each more hopeless than the last. Thirteen years ago in the ballot I got a nomination to Grundy [a top stallion]. So Robin said, 'All right, but get yourself a proper mare, and if it doesn't work this time, you must give it up.'" Burdened with this make-or-break responsibility, Lady Tavistock went to the sales and promptly, some would say, took leave of her senses.

"Well, I saw this mare walking round the ring because she hadn't

made her reserve price. And she had this wonderful face; the kindest face you ever saw.'' So captivated was she by the mare's wise, kind face that she actually didn't notice that the animal had a deformed hoof: a club foot. "And I honestly was not conscious of buying her. I just know that the hammer fell, and it was shouted 'Lady Tavistock!', and then I panicked. Robin had said I could only buy one mare, and that was it; and here I'd bought this creature . . ." She vainly tried to resell her. "So I hid her from Robin for months. He didn't know she was in Suffolk, at a stables near our old home there. Then she had her foal, and it was Pit Stop, who fetched £1,800. I'd paid 2,100 guineas for Mrs Moss, so straight away we were nearly out of the wood, and I could tell Robin she existed. Then I sent her to the stallion Sharpen Up, and the foal Socks Up made £10,000 as a yearling . . . then to Sharpen Up again the next year, and she had Pushy."

Pushy won—among other things—the Queen Mary Stakes in 1980. Since then, Mrs Moss has produced six more foals, each of them magnificent. Her line has produced ten individual winners, and three of her sons are at stud: Precocious, undefeated winner of five races before he retired injured at two years old; Krayyan, who was sold for £150,000 as a yearling and is now at the Irish National Stud; and the extraordinary Jupiter Island, who won the 1986 Japan Cup in Tokyo and became the fastest British horse anywhere over one and a half miles, doing it in two minutes twenty-five seconds. Already Mrs Moss's grandchildren are beginning to win. And not one of the foals has ever reproduced the club foot.

And that is how, single-handed, Mrs Moss founded the fortunes of the Bloomsbury Stud at Woburn and made her mistress so glowingly, transparently, obsessively happy about it all. The stud now occupies the eighteenth-century farm buildings on the estate; it continues to pay its own way handsomely, and to expand. "Which returns the estate to an old tradition: Derby winners were bred here in the eighteenth century, you know." There are now 280 acres of fenced paddocks, and Mrs Moss has a fine private paddock and a barn the size of a small ballroom for her and her latest foal.

"She deserves absolutely anything. I spent more on vets' bills for her foot last year than she cost me originally, because she has had laminitis and needs a special shoe every two weeks; but I'd gladly spend three times the money, even when she retires. All you can see here, all of it, rests on her back. She changed my life, Mrs Moss; more than anything ever could have changed anybody's life."

Running Woburn, with its endless demands and administrative complexity, was not Lady Tavistock's choice, only her duty; it was Mrs Moss's astonishing talent for producing winners which made the great estate into the natural centre of her life.

She doesn't, surprisingly, ride herself. "I am a frightened rider. I was a Thelwell-pony child, rode at gymkhanas but never very bravely; after I married I completely lost my nerve. I don't like the idea of an excitable horse taking off with me." The whole charm of her involvement with horses is in breeding for excellence; in the curious blend of science and instinct, psychology and genetics and gambler's luck, which is the eternal fascination of a racing stud. "I see every foaling, I think you can learn a lot at that moment about the foal's potential. I put 'Equine Midwife' on my passport, actually."

Someone offered a huge, unrepeatable sum for Mrs Moss and her mysterious talent, even though she probably has only a couple more foals in her. No sale. "I was disgusted. The big money has taken all the fun out of racing. Besides, I wouldn't sell her. Not for anything." She also pursues a confident policy of avoiding hugely priced sires and sending her mares to "decent, value for money stallions. People were really shocked when I sent Mrs Moss to a £5,000 stallion, which is cheap, instead of Northern Dancer for a $950,000 nomination."

Palm Springs, Mrs Moss's latest offering to the eager flat-racing world, was careering round a girl groom who hung on to her rein with grim, practised doggedness. Mrs Moss herself, ears pricked forward, walked with relative sedateness on her bandaged foot, as her mistress led her up the gentle slopes beside the Woburn lake. We had decided to take a picture of Mrs Moss dominating the Abbey, and the foal had to come too. Mrs Moss frisked a little on the way up the slope. "She has a very good figure, for eighteen years old. Look at her back. Wouldn't think she was expecting her thirteenth foal." The mare jerked suddenly at her mistress, looking round for the foal. "Oh, you are—*strong*—" panted Lady Tavistock, hanging on tight.

"But that's her charm," says the stud groom nearby, watching the pair critically. "That strength. She puts herself together after a foal, that fast. I've never seen anything like it. A real individual, Mrs Moss."

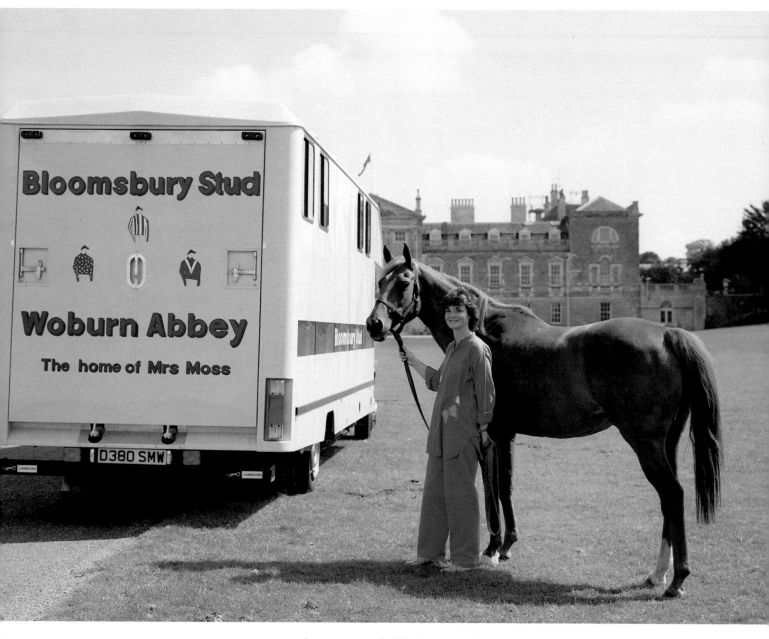

At the gates of Woburn Abbey there is a big sign for the thousands of visitors to see as they arrive:

WOBURN ABBEY
HOME OF THE DUKES OF BEDFORD FOR 300 YEARS

But the Marchioness has bought a brand-new horsebox. It is painted in the Russell family's ancient racing colours, purple and white; and on the rear door is another legend altogether:

WOBURN ABBEY
HOME OF MRS MOSS

She's taken over, all right.

THE ARTIST'S MODEL:

Annette Yarrow and Petra

She may be grazing sedately in a paddock on the edges of the New Forest, with a shaggy local pony and a stout retired cob alongside her, but Petra the Arab mare has a bloodline romantic beyond her companions' wildest dreams. Her proper name is Halaba; by Sheman out of Helaima; and, through ancestors with romantic names like Shottifa and Sahirah of the Storm, she traces her family back to Hagar, the journey-mare of the passionate Victorian Arabist and poet, Wilfred Scawen Blunt, who wrote:

> *. . . For you I rode,*
> *My horse a thing of wings, myself a God.*

Petra carries her breeding in her delicate dished face, her coat as silky as a cat's, her flowing mane and the high proud carriage of her tail. When she moves it is with the extraordinary, dreamlike floating trot of the true Arab horse, a thing of wings.

Petra, in short, is beautiful and aristocratic and a bit of a show-off; the ideal combination of attributes for a career as an artist's model, which is precisely what she is. She was bred by the gifted artist Meg Steven, and drawn and painted many times as a foal; as a wild, unbroken three-year-old on her owner's death, she was schooled by Barbara Price, and then bought seven years ago by the sculptor Annette Yarrow. Annette, in close collaboration with her husband, the photographer John Elliott, had a glamorous and important commission, for which Petra's co-operation was essential.

"We had gone over to Jordan at the invitation of Queen Noor, to make a bronze of King Hussein's favourite riding horse. It was a very hard job to do, we spent three weeks working on it, literally in a hotel bedroom, but he was delighted. After that, we had an idea." The idea was to commemorate in bronze the Bedouin heritage, rapidly being lost under westernization. "I mean the time when it used to be just a man on his horse with his rifle, and he was king of the world." Annette had a vision of a rearing Arab mare, tough and bone-hard, carrying a tribesman in flowing robes, rifle held aloft in triumph. Back home in Hampshire, she made a rough sketch model of her idea, and took it back to Jordan. "The King carried it into the throne room with his secretary, one on each end of the crate, and opened it. He said straight away that he would like us to do it. I said, what size? And he said, 'Life size, I think, and we will put it in front of the new Houses of Parliament.' " But King Hussein also said that Annette must have a real Arab horse as a model. It had to be a mare, because the tribesmen used to use mares in preference to stallions as they were quieter on sudden raids; and Annette, as a lifetime horsewoman (once she was Champion Amateur Jockey of South India on the flat), felt strongly that she must find a real, hardy, lean and wiry Arab rather than the slightly effete and chubbily prettified versions which often find their way into the showrings of the West.

She found Petra, and the partnership has blossomed beautifully. After long labour involving eight tons of plasticine, a welded armature made by John, a quantity of wire mesh and a great deal of

to-ing and fro-ing about the precise authenticity of saddlery and gun, a lifesize Petra with Bedouin rider now prances in front of the Jordanian Houses of Parliament. It is officially called "Memorial to a Soldier of the Arab Revolution", but the Elliotts still think of it as "The Bedouin Heritage". But Petra's modelling career continues: several more versions of her are in the studio, hurtling round an imaginary corner in a series of breathtaking bronzes for Asprey's; aspects of Petra's anatomy appear and disappear, ghost-like, on a score of other equestrian statues in the workshop.

"She's perfect as a model. I keep her very fit, ride her and lunge her constantly. When I have an idea in my mind, I let her out in the field and just stand, with John, and watch her and watch her. I have to fill my eye with the real thing; he takes photographs of certain moments in the horse's movement, which I can use, but sometimes he has to take those away and just let me watch Petra moving. She'll just go round and round in circles until you tell her to stop; you get all the action you want, easily." Petra's white mane flows, her high tail swishes, her clean limbs swing around the field; Annette and John, sculptor and photographer, feast upon her.

"Then I work, mainly with bare hands, building up the model; but if ever a detail escapes me, I just go out and see her. If I want to

know, for instance, exactly how the muscles look when a leg is raised at a certain angle, I just go and pick up her leg and look at it for as long as I like. She doesn't mind."

Annette Yarrow is a painstaking realist in her sculpture. Look closely at the tiny raised hoof of one of her bronze statuettes, and you will find it has a correctly shaped frog in it. She claims never to cheat over the line of a muscle for the sake of artistic effect, and studies the anatomical drawings of Stubbs. "Some artists fudge it, and say, 'That's how I see it'; but I never cheat anatomically. It helps to groom horses; I've been doing it for fifty-five years, and I just get a feeling of how things go. When I was about to model the final surface on the Bedouin Heritage statue, which was life-sized, I went and groomed Petra first, then put oil and turps on my hands, and took a blower hairdryer, and just groomed the statue's surface, the plasticine, into shape with the same movements." Artistically, too, this painstaking accuracy pays off. Using her own eye and experience, and John's brilliant photographs of the horse in motion, Annette often captures a line of muscles in a fleeting moment of coming-into-tension, a moment so brief in real life that the eye could not catch it. The result is that the eye, seeing the statue, cannot accept that it is not moving. Some of Annette's effects are uncanny; her horses give an overwhelming illusion of being about to leap off the table and gallop hell-for-leather across the floor at knee height. "You see, horses get themselves into attitudes which, unless you photographed and sculpted them, you simply wouldn't see—the angle seems so steep, the leg so oddly placed. But it's real."

The reality of her horses appeals to horsemen. Princess Anne was delighted to examine the sculpture of herself on her champion eventer Doublet, an early piece of work: "We crawled around the floor together discussing whether the bottoms were the right size, and so on . . ." And a good proportion of her customers, both through Asprey's and directly, are horsemen and women wanting to immortalize one special animal. But it is also part of a revived school of animal realism, free from the artful art-school trickeries and semi-abstracts of recent years. Annette, after all, only began sculpting by playing with her children's clay when she was at home with four of them. "I suddenly caught a likeness of the baby's head. I went on from there. I've always just asked for technical advice about materials and casting and so on; but I suppose I learnt by myself. And meeting John helped, with the way we work together with photographs and models." As for Petra, whose ancestress was celebrated in verse, she is immortal in bronze many times over. And the flesh-and-blood line goes on, too: she is due to foal this year. Another star, one suspects, is born.

THE CART-HORSES:

Charlie Pinney's Ardennes Pair

If you think that Charlie Pinney is trying to turn the clock back and prettify the scenery by using cart-horses and producing farm machinery for them to pull, you couldn't be more wrong. He is strictly practical.

"The cart-horse is in a terrible dilemma," he sighs. "On the one hand there's the romantic appeal, on the other there's an undoubted use for them on a farm, but it's bloody hard work. I'm into making horses earn their living. We've got to earn the crispies. I'm not for all that standing around in a smock with a piece of straw in your mouth."

Charlie's business revolves around what he describes as "taking the back end of a tractor and fitting it to the back end of a horse". Because he is no romantic, he is not foolish enough to think that horses will ever plough the land again on a large scale; it would be too slow and need too many men. But for certain jobs, horses genuinely win on economic grounds. "It's stupid to use a 100 h.p. tractor to deliver three bales of hay to a field." He spits the words out contemptuously. "A horse is ideal for a job like that. Jobs with a low power requirement like harrowing or rolling. Why dismiss a source of power? Especially as it does little damage to the land." Hence Pinney's array of brand-new fertilizer spreaders, hay mowers, and muck-carts, which he produces and exports to developing countries which are either behind, or—looking at it another way—ahead of us when it comes to cultivating their land.

Charlie Pinney would say they were ahead. His own interest in the working horse was born out of poverty. "We had a family farm in Dorset. We were milking cows at the time and couldn't afford a tractor. So I got a horse. I paid £200 for it and a year later I had twelve of them."

As if the future of the cart-horse in general was not enough to

preach about, Pinney also finds time to be Britain's main advocate of the Ardennes breed of horses. "We went on our honeymoon in 1975 — it was before the wedding, as it happened, because we wanted to be back for the hay harvest . . . We were in France and they gave me two of them, to start up the breed in England. They actually *gave* me two. So I brought them home, and I suppose all the Ardennes in England have come from me." That original pair were resoundingly named Hautaine du Borbeau and Goguette du Borbeau.

Ardennes are big, heavy horses, but compact. They do not tower over you like the Shires, Suffolks or Clydesdales, our native breeds of cart-horse. Nor do they seem to have the conformation or spirit that might have made them stars of the showring. But they have a noble history, both on the battlefield in centuries past, and in the never-ending battle with the land. "They are quiet and sensible," says Pinney fondly. "They can get as fat as pigs on thin air." (For this reason, it must be said, they are also much loved by the horsemeat butchers of Europe.) He now keeps two on his twenty-five-acre grassland farm near Honiton in Devon. "Polly is a six-

year-old. I'd say she was an independent sort of horse. A good observer of people. I give her to lads sent to me for teaching by the Agricultural Training Board. She knows they're learners so she'll make fools of them if she can."

Charlie harnessed Polly and her son Trojan for a morning's work with the chain-harrow which they would drag up and down the field. "I don't use blinkers on my horses. Ever. They're safer without them. My horses worry about nothing. Lorries, even, don't bother them. Very often when we're working away the old horses will turn round and look at me as if to make sure I'm still with them. They couldn't do that in blinkers." Trojan is only two years old. "I always say that if a cart-horse can't be broken to harness in twenty-four hours, then it ought to be in a tin."

With this threat echoing in his mind, Trojan takes up the strain on his collar and sets off round the field with Polly, chain-harrow behind them. We come to the end of one circuit of the field, and Charlie and the horses all pause for a breath. They look wonderful, timeless, but he only says: "It seems terribly sad to me that the cart-horse should be tied up in the nostalgia business. Terribly sad."

THE HUNTER:

Captain Ronnie Wallace and Minstrel

"What you have to understand about any real foxhunting man," an ex-hunting friend explained kindly to me, "is that he is a sound horseman, but he actually prefers dogs." Captain Ronnie Wallace, Master of the Exmoor Hunt, admits that masters of foxhounds do have this reputation. "We're supposed to be chaps who are besotted by hounds and hound-work, and regard a horse as a sort of bicycle. I think, though," he adds thoughtfully, "that this attitude is a mistake."

He has been an MFH for forty-five years, is chairman of the Masters of Fox Hounds Association, and rather conspiratorially admits that hunting—including hunt politics and the national affairs of the sport—has taken up "nearly the whole" of his time for four decades. He knows everybody who takes hunting seriously, and everybody knows him. More than any other man living, perhaps, Ronnie Wallace understands the spell of those long winter days engaged in what Nancy Mitford described as: "The rushing, the scrambling, the splashing, struggling up the hills, sliding down them again, the tugging, the bucketing, the earth and the sky . . . absolute concentration, both mental and physical."

He had his own pack of beagles and terriers when he was twelve, became Master of the Eton Beagles at sixteen, and took on his first proper mastership while he was actually away fighting in World War II.

"But I didn't like the riding part of it until I was at Oxford, and acquired an old horse. A good old hunter, who knew what she was doing—it made all the difference, after ponies. This old grey mare, Silver, she taught me to ride." Since then there have been many hunters. He used to favour "a good stamp of Irish horse", with the Irish light draught-horse bloodline, strong but sparky, as favoured by the Royal Horse Artillery. "For some years I've been a heavy

chap, and you can't use a small horse for hunting unless you're a little girl of no substance. English cart-horse blood doesn't come through too well, but we've bred several fine hunting Irishmen at home. And I used to have a marvellous three-quarter-bred Irish horse called Bolster. I named him because he had legs like bolsters when I bought him!" Poor old Bolster, far more than a bicycle to the Captain, died eventually and was sadly missed. "Then I had a marvellous black and white horse that cost me £250—what was its name?—Klondike, plain sort of horse, but he could gallop!" Now, however, his two favourite horses have very superior blood in them. "They stand in the stable and boast at you, 'Do you know my grandfather won the Derby?' Both of them are grandchildren of Pinza. Remember? Sir Gordon Richards won his last Derby on Pinza." These two, Miss Dawn and Young Pretender, both suit him and his Exmoor terrain very well. "Not so much high jumping, but uphill and downhill and over streams and generally careering about." Halfway through a hunt, his second horse will be brought out, at a gentle walk, by a groom so that the Master can remount and find fresh speed. "Trouble is, once you get me on a good horse, I'm difficult to shift. My second horseman used to be this very good girl, who practically used to knock me out of the saddle." In our

picture, the Captain rides Minstrel. "Dear little horse, only just big enough for me, but marvellous for the terrain. Think he's got some Exmoor pony blood in him."

The important thing to understand about a hunting man or woman, especially a master, is that when they are out for the day they are *not* "out riding". They are hunting—thinking about the hounds, the scent, the fox, the ground, and noticing with beady eyes exactly how their neighbours are farming. The horse is underneath them all the time, but they don't want to have to think about it much. "For instance," says Ronnie Wallace, reasonably, "these eventing horses. They don't usually make good hunters because they're used to getting every instruction from their riders. They have to be, because so many obstacles built for them are really traps, so they wait for prompting all the time. But when I get to a fence or a hedge or a stream, I like a horse that makes it own arrangements." He requires, therefore, common sense, an equable temperament, and stamina, rather than flashy good looks or prissily immaculate paces. Certainly a hunter doesn't need the same showmanlike temperament as a showjumper or a dressage horse. "I rode Housewarmer, a gelding, years ago, he'd run four times in the National and never fallen, and he adored hunting. They'd tried to make him into a showjumper, but whenever he saw a ring, and a crowd, he went berserk. He got a reputation, and came to me with this amazing bit, full of rollers and things I didn't understand at all, to keep him in control. But the moment we found our first fox, he dropped his bit. Good as gold. Then I took him to Richmond for a hound parade, and he started to go berserk again, until he saw the hounds with me and calmed down." Certainly some horses seem to take to hunting with uncanny keenness, spotting foxes, watching hounds, joining in their rider's atavistic, excited eagerness. For eagerness it is: Ronnie Wallace is in his seventh decade, has had both hips replaced and served more than half his life as a master, but on his favourite subject he still sounds like a small boy with his first pack of terriers.

"Hunting, you see, is what Surtees called it, the image of war, without its guilt, and only twenty-five per cent of the danger. It's risky, every season one or two people get killed, and the hospitals in hunting country get filled up with casualties; I've broken a vertebra and got concussed a few times. But it's marvellous. Perhaps a little less full of joy than it was when I was young; the countryside isn't the same, for one thing. But wonderful. I mean, if you ask us, we'll all tell you that hunting is a good thing because it gives employment, because it controls foxes, because it promotes conservation interests in the countryside. But actually we really do it because we think it is the most marvellous thing in the world."

THE STEEPLECHASER:
Bob Champion and Aldaniti

When Aldaniti, ridden by Bob Champion, ran in the 1981 Aintree Grand National it was not only the punters who willed them on. Everyone wanted Bob Champion and Aldaniti to win, and when they did a cheer ran round the world. In that moment these two became one of the great partnerships. Between them they have defied probability and history, and beaten injury and cancer as well as that one year's field of hopeful Grand National steeplechasers. They have become a legend. Bob Champion, like most jockeys, is not a man to gush sentimentally about a former "ride", but admits, "You have your favourites. He was one."

They first raced together in 1977 when Bob, a tough and experienced jump jockey, joined trainer Josh Gifford's stable and rode Aldaniti in the Hennessy Gold Cup for his owners, Nick and Valda Embiricos. Bob had known Aldaniti since he was a four-year-old, and remembers him as "A very strong horse, in his early days. He took a lot of holding. But he was always very good over fences, with that low head carriage which usually means a good jumper. He was a very good ride, but he did take a strong hold of you." The horse clouted the second fence, and chipped two pieces of bone off his pastern on one hind leg. This was discovered afterwards, but meanwhile he had raced on to finish third. "He was off for a long time, more than six months, in his box resting. But he wasn't put off. Some horses don't come back to their old selves after being off for injury, but he did. In a way, I reckon racehorses have got just so many miles on the clock: the more races they do, the less years of running they have. With all his injuries, Aldaniti only ever ran about twenty-one times, which is very little in eight years." He admired the horse's spirit in finishing that Hennessy so

successfully: "I suppose it's the adrenalin. When you're heated up, you don't feel the injuries. You only see that a horse is hurt when he cools down."

Bob won other races on Aldaniti, and came to think of him as "my ride". But in 1979, after a savage racing injury to one of his testicles, Bob was diagnosed as having a tumour. And so began a long and doubtful battle against cancer, and against the weakening, painful hardships of the various cancer treatments themselves. Just as Aldaniti had suffered weary confinement to his box for all those months while his leg injuries mended, so Bob Champion, the active horseman, had to live for months in hospital beds and in a state of convalescent weakness.

"During all that time I had to give myself goals. If I didn't have something to look forward to, I'd have shot myself." So he formed the idea—some say the obsession—that he would one day be cured, and would win the Grand National on Aldaniti.

"I'd always thought he was a decent horse, very much the National type. A National winner has got to jump, and be a stayer, and have speed. And he had all three." Bob came out of the Royal Marsden Hospital in January 1980. He had no hair, weighed only nine stone—a cruel irony for a jockey who had spent his life hitherto fighting the usual battle to keep his weight down to ten stone—and could barely walk. Aldaniti was his target for regaining fitness: nobody but he should ride that horse in the National. His last treatments wore on and, in the event, he missed the 1980 National. He kept his resolve, though, and, to the startled amazement of the racing world, was riding winners again by the end of 1980. Aldaniti remained in the background. "I only sat on him four times between the time I was in hospital and the time we won the National. I schooled him over three fences before Ascot, then rode one race which he won, then rode him on the morning of the National and in the National itself." Each time, his faith in the horse was renewed.

"I still thought he could win. I say now that I thought it was a certainty, but I wasn't ever confident until we got past that winning post. For one thing, a jockey never should be that confident; for another, I knew that his old injuries might come back to trouble him. His legs aren't the greatest, he's had three bad injuries." Bob's own illness was forgotten in his burning hope for Aldaniti. At 3.20 p.m. the thirty-nine runners moved up to the starting tape, and the hospital dream was minutes away from fulfilment. At the first fence the horse nearly fell. "I thought we had gone," Bob wrote later in his autobiography, *Champion's Story*. "What a waste for both of us. He was on the ground, down. His nose and knees scraping the grass. We'd had it." He rose, somehow, and "found a leg"; scraped

Page 147 Bob Champion and Aldaniti at the culmination of a charity ride at Aintree before the 1987 Grand National.

himself on the second fence, jibbed briefly at a startling ditch, then found his form at last. "I sat on him, a complete passenger. Although he was pulling hard, he knew what to do each time we reached a fence." In this most dangerous, crowded, unpredictable of races, Aldaniti poured himself over fence after fence, his wondering jockey beginning to think that the dream he had nursed of rising from illness and defeat to win the National was actually likely to come true. "I'd never sat on anything that jumped like Aldaniti. He was like a cat, so fast, so sure, and loving every minute of it. He's my type of horse. So genuine and honest. He would never shirk from anything." And he won. In the last few furlongs, Spartan Missile challenged from behind, but with his tongue out, weary and determined, Aldaniti shot past the finishing post alone.

It was the sort of day that makes a legend: it has already made a successful film. In the months after that Grand National, Bob set up a charitable fund for research into the causes and treatment of cancer in young adults, the Bob Champion Cancer Trust. Aldaniti undertook a fundraising sponsored walk of 250 miles from Epsom to Aintree in 1987, with Bob riding the last mile, and other distinguished horsemen and women, including the Princess Royal and the Duchess of York, taking intermediate stages. The horse took the long walk and the frequent changes of rider with stoicism and good humour, and the Trust has now raised over £2 million for research and for treatment at the Royal Marsden. Bob Champion—now a successful trainer in his own right—gives it unstinting time and co-operation. But in some ways, he did more to encourage cancer patients in those tense minutes at Aintree in 1981 than he will ever be able to do again.

As for Aldaniti, his racing days are past, but his scarred eighteen-year-old legs continue to hold out well. Back with his owners, he is ridden and hunted regularly. "I don't like to see racehorses turned out to grass, it's cruel," says Bob. "If they've always been in training, why shouldn't they do different things? They enjoy it. Aldaniti's quite happy. I like to see him again sometimes, whenever we do something together for the Trust. I like the old horse. He's been good to me."

THE STABLE FAVOURITE:

Brian Higham and the Duke of Beaufort's Lord

When I walked into the tackroom of the largest private hunting stable in the world, I glanced at the clock that hung on the dark, panelled wall. It had stopped. It might have happened only yesterday, or a hundred years ago, for this is a slice of English aristocratic life that has been untouched by the passing of time, the upheavals of war, or frivolous changes in fashion. "Just look at it!" said Brian Higham, the stud groom. (He is really the stable manager, but prefers the traditional title of stud groom as he thinks it is more "in keeping".) He gazes around him, conscious of the oddity of these, his everyday surroundings. "Who could really afford to run a place like this? There's over forty horses here, hunting four days a week in the season. We polish all the brass on the headcollars and even the brass on the catches of the stable doors." After thirty years here, he is still awestruck by the majesty of this building and its ways. I noticed lengths of heated black pipe crossing the tackroom floor. "We dry the saddles over those if they come back wet from hunting. There's about fifty saddles in here. We like them to be linen-lined if possible." He shrugged his shoulders. "Who could afford it?"

It is a rhetorical question, of course. It is the Duke of Beaufort who affords all this. His home is at Badminton, and this stable, this temple of worship to the hunting of the fox, is his too. "Look at the weathervanes," continued Brian. "They've all got the fox on top but, unlike a weathervane with a cock, the fox points away from the wind not into it. That's because a fox will always run with the wind to hide his scent." With fox-like cunning, such hunting details have been built into every corner of this massive building. Badminton *is* horses: the late Duke of Beaufort made sure of that. He kept up the hunting tradition that his father had laid down, and added to it the world-famous three-day event. When he died four years ago, his cousin, the present Duke, not only inherited estate, hunt and event and a great deal of equestrian *noblesse oblige*, he also inherited Brian Higham. Anyone who is anyone in hunting knows Brian. Although he insists he is a servant, he is closer to the master's table than many. He proudly showed me his Christmas card signed "Charles & Diana", and he was invited to *the* wedding.

We went from the tackroom into his office. It is lined with the same dark panelling, but instead of the aroma of leather it has the clinical odour of horse-liniment and kaolin poultices from the first-aid cupboard. On the wall is a map of the area hunted by the Beaufort. It is not new; actually, it is stamped *War Office Edition*.

"My job is quite simple. I have to produce horses that are sound and fit for the masters, the hunt staff and the guests. It's all down to good management in the end. I insist on cleanliness. You can tell a yard by its muck heap, that's what I always say. And there's no penny-pinching here. If I want best linseed, I just order best linseed. I've only got the Duke to answer to." He has a tall wooden desk in his office, like something a Dickensian clerk might have written at; I was slightly disappointed to find no quill pen.

All runs smoothly here, as it always did. The present Duke hunts regularly, for preference on his favourite horse Lord, but the old Duke of Beaufort was indisputably a hard act to follow. "He was still hunting at eighty-four and he'd be up and dressed with his stock on at 7.30, ready to go. He was a man of great principle, a very good horseman. But he lived in a world of his own. I don't think he even knew the pound had gone up." Brian led me along the corridors of the cavernous and spotless stables, and showed me at the end of the row of twenty horses a box marked "Jupiter". Jupiter was the old Duke's favourite, given by the new Duke as a present to Brian Higham.

Brian's own family were coachmen and gamekeepers. "I rode farm horses in Yorkshire when I was fourteen, and came here when I was twenty-five as what's called 'second man'. When the Duke hunted, I used to follow with a spare horse so he could swap over when the first horse got tired. I'd then take the first one home slowly. I did that for seven years." Now, with an experience of hunters that is unlikely to be matched by any groom in the business, he finds that even the job of buying horses for the Badminton stables often falls to him. "I always used to say the price of a good hunter is the same as the price of a Mini car. When a Mini was five hundred quid, so was a hunter. Now you're talking about three to six thousand. You can tell a lot about a hunter from its head. It's got to have a bold eye, and be clever. And tough, too. Hunting is getting harder. There used to be a lot more grassland to hunt over, now it's arable fields and that's harder on the horses. I also think we've bred from too many bad mares. You can't breed from mice and get rats!"

Knowing every horse, its condition, and its ways is at the centre of Brian's job: when we watched the horses at exercise, he would not leave until they had each got into a canter under his critical eye. "It's not a glamorous job. It's long hours in the winter and more mundane than eventing, to a lot of people. But I believe in hunting. It's a way of life and it's the backbone of rural life. I'm only a paid servant, but I'm proud of it; proud to say I've been associated with the old Duke, and the new one."

There is no retirement age for stud grooms. Like the horses they tend, they can stay on as long as they are sound in wind and limb and earn their keep. Which must be a consoling reflection to the Beaufort family, for, not unlike the grand old Duke, Brian Higham is going to be a hard act to follow.

THE LADY'S HACK:

Margaret Howard and Tara-el-Hacene

Ever since she was a child, there was a tin box in Margaret Howard's kitchen labelled HORSE FUND. "I always wanted a horse, and had a few seven-and-sixpenny lessons round the park. But it was a suburban childhood, and I never did much." She grew up horseless, and came to work for the BBC, where she is one of BBC Radio's best-known voices from *Pick of the Week* on Radio 4, and from the late, enormously popular *Letterbox* on the World Service. And, oddly enough, it was the BBC which eventually led to the fulfilment of her childhood dream, and the final spending of the Horse Fund.

"It was ten years ago, when I was a reporter on *The World at One*, doing a tough news job. I was working with a crowd of hard-bitten journalists, who spent a lot of time drinking and smoking and eating and just sitting getting fat. This was before the great Jane Fonda health boom, but there was already a feeling around that one somehow should be more fit than that. I began to feel unhealthy. And I needed to get out and do something that wasn't BBC, because if you're not careful, programmes like that can absorb you completely and give you very little back." While she was pondering, some friends asked her to come and having riding lessons with them and their five-year-old daughter. In the event, Margaret was the only one to stick at it; completely hooked again, besotted, fulfilling her old longing for a horse.

"I was a terrible coward, thirty-nine years old and much too stiff to want to fall off. My teacher took me in hand, and then one day led me to a field where there was this sprightly young chestnut leaping around like a mad thing. She said, 'That's the horse for you!' I said that I wouldn't even sit on that thing, but she insisted."

So Margaret bought Tara-el-Hacene, a graceful part-Arab mare with a long back and an unruly temperament, and found herself "very over-horsed. Tara was much too young for me, and I could have caused her damage; but my teacher just said 'Leave her alone,

she's a clever little horse,' and she did keep me out of trouble. She knows that she's in charge of things, but she's a kind creature, and when she runs away, which she does a lot, she goes in a straight line. Doesn't try to brush or swerve me off. The trouble is, in ten years I have learned quite a lot, and she doesn't admit it. Still thinks she's the boss. When we're out hacking, suddenly she'll snatch the reins and head off in another direction, and the trouble is she's usually quite right."

Margaret—whose broadcasting work is enormously controlled and disciplined—seems to revel in the contrast provided by her wilful mare. "Oh, she's taken ten years off me. She's the softest, gentlest creature to handle; she even puts up with my deaf old dog. I've even put him on her back, she doesn't mind. And she never bites. I had one horse on approval, a very good horse, but he bit me right on my front. I put him straight back in the trailer, and said that I just wouldn't have a horse that bit me. The owner was quite surprised that I minded, said that the horse did it a lot, and you just had to dodge. But I prefer not to be bitten. The only thing Tara doesn't like much is men; I think she must once have encountered the sort of tough, positive man who said, 'I'll sort that horse out,' and bullied her. Women, I think, not only ride lighter in the saddle but they're more yielding than men; they tend to think around a problem rather than trying to move in and take total control. Tara likes women best."

Part of the progress Margaret has made is that she now jumps regularly—the mare over-jumps spectacularly and with glee—has been in local shows and small cross-country events, and is taking dressage lessons. "She loves shows because she's a show-off horse, behaves herself when there's a crowd; she's good at jumping, but very wild, does it her way, twisting anyhow she likes. The dressage is good because, for a change, I am in complete control. It's good for her. I'm still having lessons, every Thursday, because I think if you don't have formal lessons you never get better, and I want to be better, partly because I want to be safer."

One aspect of their partnership which has not changed is that the horse doesn't like to be caught. Margaret doesn't keep her at a full livery stables, but in a more informal setting: "I catch her, groom her, tack up, feed her afterwards and clean the tack." This has the disadvantage that it is quite possible for Margaret, a busy single working woman, to drive thirty-five miles down from London, and find herself unable to ride because Tara simply won't be caught. "I'll try everything—titbits, sugar, standing still . . . once I got so furious with her for cantering around escaping me that I started throwing things, buckets, branches, everything, saying, 'OK, you want to canter, you canter'—and keeping her on the go for an

hour, like a sort of free lunging session. I exercised her, all right, without ever getting a hand on her!" Usually, however, the rider's will and a supply of titbits triumph, and the pair ride out together across the Surrey hills on long contented hacks in company with friends. It has been a good association. For one thing, Margaret Howard is now fighting fit, from the riding and the stable work — "All that bending and stretching with hay, and grooming, the same movements I'd have done mirthlessly and boringly in an aerobics class!" — but she has also found endless stimulation and challenge in her sparky and unbiddable mount.

"Starting to learn at my advanced age, if I'd taken sensible advice, I would have got a big steady horse, what they call a 'schoolmaster'. But with a horse like that, I would have got cocky, and thought how good I was and stopped trying. My horse has never, ever, allowed me to feel that I'm good at it. So I get better. I've had some hairy times, but I'm glad it was her, and not some old plug of a Patent Safety Horse. We get on together. She keeps me out of mischief."

Margaret stares mistily at her collection of pictures of Tara-el-Hacene. "Really, we were such unpromising material ten years ago; I was old and cowardly, she was young and wild. But we have made something of a partnership. That's a thing to be glad of."

THE CEREMONIAL HORSE:

Sir John Miller and Rio

*All the King's horses and all the King's men
Couldn't put Humpty together again.*

This event must clearly have occurred before Sir John Miller's time as Crown Equerry. In the years that he was in charge of the royal horses, it is difficult to imagine that any horse or man was allowed to fail at any duty, or put one well-blacked hoof or boot out of place, let alone jib at a meagre task like resurrecting a fallen egg. Humpty Dumpty, you feel, would have been all right with Sir John in charge. He is now retired, and talked to me at his family home in Oxfordshire, where visitors are greeted disconcertingly by a large stuffed Kodiak bear, apparently carrying a gun, although the hall was dim and I was too startled to take it all in thoroughly on the way through. He gave me tea and toast, and remembered.

"Of course, it wasn't only the horses. I was also responsible for the cars and duties of the chauffeurs," he pointed out fair-mindedly.

"Which gave you more trouble, horses or cars?" I asked.

After a long pause for thought he said, "I don't suppose either gave me much bother, really." If they had, the whole world would have known about it. On a State occasion, in a dignified procession, it is a *sine qua non* that the Queen's horses shall behave with perfect manners.

"I remember Princess Anne's wedding. One of the greys in a team of four that was pulling the royal coach bucked when he heard the Gurkha band strike up as it crossed Horse Guards Parade. The horse's back legs got tangled in the traces" [the leather straps that take the weight of the carriage]. "I could have stopped the procession there and then, and got it sorted out, but it would have been 'Wedding Disaster' headlines in the newspapers. So I let

him trot on with all the leather between his back legs. No one noticed."

This particular horse, Rio, is actually a bit of a favourite. He is, at twenty-two, the second oldest horse in the Royal Mews and the one on which Sir John chose to be photographed for his official retirement picture. "He was a lively horse, 'gay', if I may use that word these days. He's of the Oldenburg breed, a heavy type of horse, a European ceremonial horse. He knew my voice. I only had to tell him to stand still, and he obeyed immediately." Wise horse.

As if thirty of the Queen's horses were not enough responsibility for one man to bear, Sir John Miller was also in charge of the men who tended them and the buildings in which horses and men are housed. They call these the Royal Mews: they lie at the back of Buckingham Palace. Here live the grooms, saddlers, carpenters and carriage-builders who keep the world's most regal equestrian show on the road. "It's a sort of village, the Mews," said Sir John. I asked him how he saw his position as Crown Equerry in relation to it. "Commanding Officer," he said. Then paused, "Or perhaps the village squire."

Whatever he was, he certainly brought to the job a wealth of horsemanship. There is little that can be done with horses that John Miller has not mastered. He hunted from the age of ten, took up three-day eventing when Badminton first started, and was in the 1952 British three-day event team at the Helsinki Olympics. As for carriage-driving: "I took it up during the war when there was no petrol for cars. I still have the dog-cart I used to ride around in. I was part of the first ever driving competition, held in 1970. In fact, Rio was part of my four-horse team then."

Sir John is also past-president of the Coaching Club, an exclusive and long-established group of gentlemen who all have to own a private coach and four horses. It is said to be the most difficult club in the world to join. Sir John did not disagree. "Money will not buy membership. There are no social criteria except perhaps, shall I say, behaviour." And with that, the subject was closed. The Coaching Club doesn't even talk about itself much, to outsiders. The only time the public gets a glimpse of its fabulous scope and skill, of coaches and drivers and perfect horses, is on their annual picnic—if that is not too lowly a word—when they drive from the Royal Stables at Windsor, through Windsor Great Park to the Royal Enclosure at Ascot. On that day you might see the teams of the Duke of Edinburgh, Sir John Miller, John Parker and the cream of the driving world, human and animal, all polished and burnished and groomed to a hair.

Of the royal processions, Sir John remembers with most pleasure and pride "The Queen's Silver Jubilee, in 1977. It was marvellous. I rode in the procession with the Prince of Wales and the Duke of Beaufort, who was then Master of the Queen's Horse. I rode Burmese, the famous old mare which the Queen herself used to ride at Trooping the Colour." But he could have chosen from any of a dozen other memorable royal milestones of the latter half of the twentieth century; major events at which he was one of the team which ensured that the horses got young royal brides and bridegrooms smoothly, and beautifully, to the church on time. There was Princess Anne's wedding to Captain Mark Phillips; Prince Charles's brilliant wedding to Lady Diana Spencer, which broke with tradition by using St Paul's Cathedral and so gave the masters of Horse and of Ceremonies the task of taking the carriages right down the Strand and Fleet Street, crossing half of London; most recently, Prince Andrew's exuberant marriage to Sarah Ferguson. There was the Queen's silver wedding anniversary, the Queen Mother's eightieth birthday, and dozens of minor state processions to honour visiting heads of State. In all of them Sir John, and in his due place Rio, have been involved.

But is it not all coming to an end? International terrorism has driven most other monarchs and heads of State behind the dark bulletproof glass of black limousines, to be glimpsed only fleetingly by their people, and represented by the semi-anonymous flutter of a flag on the bonnet. Won't our own Royal Family, eventually and reluctantly, abandon the horses and carriages, the openness, nodding and waving and smiling, of another age's fairytales? Suggest as much to Sir John and he fires up immediately.

"I think that the future of the horse-drawn procession is more

secure than it has ever been. The Prince of Wales's wedding made an impact world-wide. I doubt whether it would have been the same if it had just been a long crocodile of black limousines. In carriages, the Royal Family can be seen and that is what the people want. I really can't see the Household Cavalry escorting black cars, can you? Not in this country."

He paused to take a refreshing look around his sitting-room, adorned with pictures of his favourite horses, a picture of his father in the uniform of a colonel of the Scots Greys, and a youthful portrait of the Queen.

"No, we've put on some good things in recent years. We have a way of doing things in Britain. We just carry on."

THE GYPSY'S FRIEND:

George Brown and Billy

Billy is three, but George Brown, not much of a man for counting, couldn't tell me how old he is himself. He is from a family of English travelling people, who no longer live on the road. For it is not, now, cheap or easy to be a gypsy in England: casual work is hard to come by; police and local authorities chase you off sites which were once open; horses can no longer be grazed freely on verges and commons; and fuel for the big, flashy caravans which most travellers now favour is expensive. So George lives in County Durham—he couldn't remember exactly where, just said, "Aaaaye, home, County Durham"—and gets by with "a bit of hawking, a bit of firewood-selling". Billy is the first horse he has ever had; he bought him unbroken, and sorted him out himself. "Not too baaad. I never broke one in afore, but it was not all that baad." There seems to be a decent relationship between them, Billy drooping his black head affectionately over George, George hissing at Billy through his teeth. Billy is not yet fit for heavy loads, but successfully pulls an old, lightish, flat-cart for the hawking business. "He's done that a canny bit, aaye." George's ambition is to have a proper, cloth-topped little caravan and live in it.

We found George and Billy on their summer holiday week, on the way to Appleby Fair in Cumbria, a two-day journey from home. George rides the cart, on the level, but "I do walk, up the hills, aaaye." The flat-cart may look, to a casual motorist flashing by, as if it is loaded with rubbish; in fact, the rubbish is the carefully assembled component parts of George's "tent". There are a couple of old wooden benches, a box, a roll of foam carpet underlay and a ragged tarpaulin. The underlay and the tarpaulin are spread over the box, weighted with stones, and keep the interior dry for George to sleep in, wrapped in a tangle of old blankets, while Billy is staked out to graze alongside.

At the other end of the scale, there is no shortage of conspicuous wealth among the travelling people. At the gypsy gathering at Appleby George will pull up on the grass alongside £40,000 trailers, gleaming with chrome decoration, crammed with ornate Angelica Kauffman-style plates and fairground-rococo decorations. Billy the black pony will graze as an equal next to horses who pull magnificent modern reproduction gypsy caravans lined with pink ruched satin and painted with roses on every vacant surface, all clean as a new pin, with yellow canaries swinging in cages and neatly lashed bottles of butane gas for cooking. George will throw his logs together, and sit under the stars, eating his supper amid the fragrant smoke without undue envy. The carpet underlay "keeps the wet out, aaaye". And Billy is always there, for company.